HOLT
2
SPANISH

¡Ven conmigo!®

Activities for Communication

HOLT, RINEHART AND WINSTON

A Harcourt Classroom Education Company

Austin · New York · Orlando · Atlanta · San Francisco · Boston · Dallas · Toronto · London

Contributing Writers:

Herlinda James

Felicia Kongablc

Amy Propps

Laura Olson

Anne Quishuis

Cover Photo/Illustration Credits
Group of students: Marty Granger/HRW Photo; tostada recipe: Annette Cable/Clare Jett & Assoc.

¡VEN CONMIGO! is a trademark licensed to Holt, Rinehart and Winston, registered in the United States of America and/or other jurisdictions.

Printed in the United States of America

ISBN 0-03-065542-0

1 2 3 4 5 6 7   066   03 02 01

Contents

SITUATION CARDS

To the Teacher

Oral communication is the most challenging language skill to develop and test. The *¡Ven conmigo! Activities for Communication* book helps students to develop their speaking skills and gives them opportunities to communicate in many different situations. The Communicative Activities and Situation Cards provide a variety of information-gap activities, role-plays, and interviews to assist students with the progression from closed-ended practice to more creative, open-ended use of Spanish. The Realia reproduces authentic documents to provide students with additional reading practice using material written by and for native speakers. Included with the Realia are teaching suggestions and student activities showing how to integrate the four skills and culture into your realia lesson. With the focus on dialogue and real-life context, the activities in this book will help your students achieve the goal of genuine interaction.

Each chapter of *Activities for Communication* provides:

- **Communicative Activities** In each of the twelve chapters, three communicative, pair-work activities encourage students to use Spanish in realistic conversation, in settings where they must seek and share information. The activities provide cooperative language practice and encourage students to take risks with language in a relaxed, uninhibiting, and enjoyable setting. The activities correspond to each **Paso** and encourage use of functions, vocabulary, and grammar presented in that chapter section. Each activity may be used upon completion of the **Paso** as a Performance Assessment, or may be recorded on audio or video tape for inclusion in students' portfolios. The activities may also be used as an informal review of the **Paso** to provide additional oral practice.

- **Realia** In each chapter there are three reproducible pieces of realia that relate to the chapter theme and reflect life and culture in Spanish-speaking countries. Finding they can read and understand documents intended for native speakers gives students a feeling of accomplishment that encourages them to continue learning. Upon completion of each **Paso**, the realia may be used to review the functions, vocabulary, and grammar presented, or may be used as additional practice at any point within the **Paso**. Along with the blackline masters of the realia you will find suggestions for using the realia in the classroom. These suggestions include a combination of activities for individual, pair, and group work and focus on the skills of listening, speaking, reading, writing, and explore authentic cultural information.

- **Situation cards** Each of the twelve chapters contains three interviews and three situations for role-playing, one per **Paso**, in blackline master form. These cards are designed to stimulate conversation and to prepare students for speaking tests. The interviews or role-playing may be used as pair work with the entire class, as activities to begin the class period, as oral performance assessments upon completion of the **Paso**, or to encourage oral practice at any point during study of the **Paso**. These conversations may be recorded as audio or video additions to students' portfolios. Because the cards may be recycled throughout the scholastic year as review of chapters already completed, students will be rewarded as they realize they are meeting goals and improving their communicative abilities. To avoid having to copy the cards repeatedly, consider mounting them on cardboard and laminating them. They may be filed for use during the year as well as for future classes.

Communicative Activities

COMMUNICATIVE ACTIVITIES

1. Situation You and your partner are casting directors for a community theater production of *The Wizard of Oz*. Each of you took notes at the auditions, and you've decided to put this information together on cards to attach to each actor's photo.

Task Ask your partner to describe the following actors. Listen to the description and complete each card by writing any missing information in the appropriate space.

MODELO A — ¿Cuántos años tiene Maribel?
B — Tiene sesenta años.
A — ¿Y cómo es ella?
B — Es alta y canosa. Tiene ojos azules. No es muy elegante, pero es buena gente.

Nombre: Maribel

Edad: 60

Apariencia: alta, canosa, ojos azules

Personalidad: no elegante, buena gente

Nombre: Eduardo

Edad: _____

Apariencia: _____

Personalidad: _____

Nombre: Rebeca

Edad: _____

Apariencia: _____

Personalidad: _____

2. Now, use the following notes to answer your partner's questions.

Nombre: Ana Edad: 15 Apariencia: de estatura mediana, pelo rizado Personalidad: cariñosa, alegre	Nombre: Andrés Edad: 30 Apariencia: muy delgado, calvo, mide dos metros Personalidad: extrovertido, le gusta bailar

3. With your partner, decide who should play the following roles. Write one or two qualities that led you to choose each actor.

Dorothy: _____

Auntie Em: _____

The Scarecrow: _____

The Cowardly Lion: _____

Communicative Activity 1-1 B

1. **Situation** You and your partner are casting directors for a community theater production of *The Wizard of Oz*. Each of you took notes at the auditions, and you've decided to put this information together on cards to attach to each actor's photo.

Task Use your notes to describe the following actors to your partner.

MODELO
A — ¿Cuántos años tiene Maribel?
B — Tiene sesenta años.
A — ¿Y cómo es ella?
B — Es alta y canosa. Tiene ojos azules. No es muy elegante, pero es buena gente.

Nombre: Eduardo	Nombre: Rebeca
Edad: 16	Edad: 20
Apariencia: bajo, pelirrojo, guapo	Apariencia: morena, bastante alta, guapa
Personalidad: un poco tímido, cómico	Personalidad: inteligente, un poco antipática

2. Now, ask your partner for the information you need to complete your cards.

Nombre: Maribel

Edad: 60

Apariencia: alta, canosa, ojos azules

Personalidad: no elegante, buena gente

Nombre: Ana

Edad: _____

Apariencia: _____

Personalidad: _____

Nombre: Andrés

Edad: _____

Apariencia: _____

Personalidad: _____

3. With your partner, decide who should play the following roles. Write one or two qualities that led you to choose each actor.

Dorothy: _____

Auntie Em: _____

The Scarecrow: _____

The Cowardly Lion: _____

Communicative Activity 1-2A

1. **Situation** You and a friend you met at camp last summer (your partner) have sent each other pictures of your families, but you forgot to write the names on the pictures. Now you're talking on the phone, telling each other who the people in the pictures are.

Task As your partner describes each photo, write the appropriate name(s) under the photo that matches the description.

MODELO   **B — Mis abuelos visitan Guatemala.**
               A — ¿Cómo se llaman tus abuelos?
               B — Se llaman Guillermo y Mona.

_____ Guillermo _____

_____ Mona _____

_____   _____   _____   _____

_____

2. Now, switch roles and use the information below to tell your partner about the photos you sent.

mi mamá (Teresa)	tocar la guitarra
yo	tomar el sol en la playa
mis padres (Miguel y Teresa), mi hermano (David) y yo	ir al cine
mis primas (Elena y Juana)	jugar al tenis

3. If your families visited each other, who would have activities in common?

               Nombres   **Actividades**

_____   _____

_____   _____

_____   _____

Nombre _____ Clase _____ Fecha _____

1. Situation You and a friend you met at camp last summer (your partner) have sent each other pictures of your families, but you forgot to write the names on the pictures. Now you're talking on the phone, telling each other who the people in the pictures are.

Task Use the following information to describe the photos you sent to your partner.

MODELO   B — **Mis abuelos visitan Guatemala.**
              A — **¿Cómo se llaman tus abuelos?**
              B — **Se llaman Guillermo y Mona.**

Guillermo
_____

Mona
_____

mis abuelos (Guillermo y Mona)	visitar Guatemala
yo	salir con amigos
mi mamá (Felicia) y mi tía Queta	tocar el piano
mi prima Marisol	leer su libro de historia y escribir su tarea
mi hermana (Mónica) y yo	jugar al tenis

2. Now, switch roles and write the names of the people in the photos your partner describes. Remember to ask for any additional information you may need.

_____   _____   _____   _____

          _____   _____

3. If your families visited each other, who would have activities in common?

                 Nombres   **Actividades**

_____   _____

_____   _____

_____   _____

Communicative Activity 1-3A

1. Situation Your school's foreign exchange committee is looking for students to greet the new exchange students and show them around for a week. The committee has information about the exchange students' likes and dislikes, and has asked the student-body president to recommend a host student with similar interests.

Task As the committee's representative, tell the president (your partner) something about one of the international students and ask for his or her recommendation for a host. Write the president's recommendation in the space provided.

MODELO A — Gabriela Muñoz juega al baloncesto. No le gusta para nada hacer la tarea. ¿A quién recomiendas?
B — Recomiendo a Violeta Martín porque le gustan los deportes y no le gusta estudiar.

nombre	actividades favoritas	qué le gusta	qué no le gusta para nada	recomendación
Gabriela Muñoz	jugar al baloncesto	trabajar en el jardín	hacer la tarea	Violeta Martín
José Espinoza	pintar	el arte	la comida italiana	
Víctor Gómez	tocar la flauta y el piano	los deportes	la música rock	
Eduardo Tarso	pasar el rato en el parque	ir al cine	mirar la televisión	

2. Now, switch roles. Search the information for a student on the list who has something in common with the exchange student you hear descibed. Give your recommendation and explain why.

nombre	actividades favoritas	qué le gusta	qué no le gusta para nada
Soledad Mercado	ir al cine	la comida vegetariana	estudiar, estar en casa
María García	estudiar	las computadoras	los deportes
Lena Cortez	preparar comidas internacionales	salir a bailar	los animales

3. Look over all the lists. Who would you be most compatible with and why?

_____

_____

Communicative Activity 1-3B

1. **Situation** Your school's foreign exchange committee is looking for students to greet the new exchange students and show them around for a week. The committee has information about the exchange students' likes and dislikes, and has asked the student-body president to recommend a host student with similar interests.

Task You're the student body president. Listen as the committee representative (your partner) describes an exchange student, then recommend a student from the chart with similar interests. Give your recommendation for a host and explain why.

MODELO   A — **Gabriela Muñoz juega al baloncesto. No le gusta para nada hacer la tarea. ¿A quién recomiendas?**
            B — **Recomiendo a Violeta Martín porque le gustan los deportes y no le gusta estudiar.**

nombre	actividades favoritas	qué le gusta	qué no le gusta para nada
Violeta Martín	hacer ejercicio	los deportes	estudiar
Roberto Pérez	montar en bicicleta	ir al cine	estar en la ciudad
Miguel Santos	jugar al tenis y nadar	la música clásica	ir al cine
Carlos Galván	dibujar	visitar museos	comer pizza

2. Now, switch roles. Tell the student-body president something about one of the international students and ask for his or her recommendation. Write the recommendation in the space provided.

nombre	actividades favoritas	qué le gusta	qué no le gusta para nada	recomendación
Cristina Sánchez	ir a los bailes	la comida china e italiana	ir al zoológico	
Sonia Echeverría	patinar y correr	las películas	la carne	
Lupe Nieves	usar la computadora	las matemáticas y la historia	los deportes	

3. Look over all the lists. Who would you be most compatible with and why?

_____

_____

Communicative Activity 2-1A

1. Situation You and your best friend (your partner) talk on the phone all the time and help each other out with your problems.

Task Listen to your friend's problems and suggest a possible solution from the choices below.

MODELO   B — **Quiero ver un video pero no tengo dinero.**
              A — **¿Por qué no ves la televisión esta noche?**

> ¿Por qué no estudias con Julia y conmigo por la mañana?
>
> ¿Qué tal si lees unas revistas?
>
> ¿Qué tal si lo lavamos para él?
>
> ¿Por qué no vienes con nosotros?
>
> ¿Por qué no haces la maleta?

2. Now, tell your partner your problems and take notes on his or her advice.

1. Estoy triste porque Janet va a Francia por un año.

   _____

2. No quiero llevar mucho dinero en mi viaje.

   _____

3. Estoy muy aburrido/a en casa.

   _____

4. Estoy de mal humor porque tengo mucha tarea.

   _____

3. How many solutions involve you and your friend working together?

   _____

Communicative Activity 2-1 B

1. Situation You and your best friend (your partner) talk on the phone all the time and help each other out with your problems.

Task Tell your partner your problems and take notes on his or her advice.

MODELO   B — Quiero ver un video pero no tengo dinero.
                A — ¿Por qué no ves la televisión esta noche?

1. Estoy enfermo/a y no puedo salir.

   _____

2. Tengo que estudiar para un examen pero estoy cansado/a.

   _____

3. Quiero ir al baile pero no tengo coche.

   _____

4. Mi padre está enfadado porque su coche está sucio.

   _____

2. Now, listen to your friend's problems and suggest a possible solution from the choices below.

¿Por qué no vas al banco por los cheques de viajero?
¿Por qué no caminas con el perro?
¿Por qué no le escribes todas las semanas?
¿Qué tal si te ayudo con la historia?   ¿Por qué no buscas la carpeta?

3. How many solutions involve you and your friend working together?

   _____

                    Holt Spanish 2 ¡Ven conmigo!, Chapter 2

Communicative Activity 2-2A

1. Situation You and your partner are hosting a birthday party for a friend, and you've divided up the tasks. Now you're finding out what's been done.

Task Look at the list of tasks your partner was supposed to do. Ask if each has been done, then check off the ones completed.

MODELO   A — ¿Ya invitaste a todos los amigos?
         B — Sí, ya invité a los amigos. (No, todavía no.)

Mi compañero/a	Yo
✓ invitar a todos los amigos	✓ decorar la sala
limpiar la casa	✓ inventar algunos juegos
ir al supermercado	✓ comprar las bebidas
hacer unas galletas	✓ ir a la tienda de música
preparar la comida	inflar los globos
encontrar las decoraciones	✓ hacer un pastel

2. Now, look at your list of tasks. You've checked off what you've done. Answer your partner's questions about each task.

MODELO   B — ¿Ya decoraste la sala?
         A — Sí, ya decoré la sala. (No, todavía no.)

3. Who completed more tasks? _____

Who still has more to do? _____

Communicative Activity 2-2B

1. Situation You and your partner are hosting a birthday party for a friend, and you've divided up the tasks. Now you're finding out what's been done.

Task Look at your list of tasks. You've checked off what you've done. Answer your partner's questions about each task.

MODELO   A — ¿Ya invitaste a todos los amigos?
                B — Sí, ya invité a los amigos. (No, todavía no.)

Yo	Mi compañero/a
✓ invitar a todos los amigos	✓ decorar la sala
✓ ir al supermercado	hacer un pastel
preparar la comida	comprar las bebidas
✓ hacer unas galletas	ir a la tienda de música
✓ encontrar las decoraciones	inventar algunos juegos
limpiar la casa	inflar los globos

2. Now, look at the list of tasks your partner was supposed to do. Ask if each has been done, then check off the ones completed.

MODELO   B — ¿Ya decoraste la sala?
                A — Sí, ya decoré la sala. (No, todavía no.)

3. Who completed more tasks? _____

Who still has more to do? _____

Communicative Activity 2-3A

1. Situation You've found a postcard of New York City.

Task Give your partner five clues to help her or him guess what city it is. If your partner asks for extra clues, go ahead and provide them.

MODELO   **A — Es una ciudad muy grande.**

1. Es una ciudad muy grande.
2. Está al lado del océano Atlántico.
3. Hay muchos rascacielos muy bonitos.
4. En esta ciudad hay una estatua muy famosa.
5. No hay montañas en la ciudad, pero sí hay un zoológico muy famoso.
6. Hace calor en el verano y mucho frío en el invierno.

2. Your partner also has a postcard and information about another city. You'll be given five clues to guess what city it is. Take notes on your partner's description. Ask your partner in Spanish for help if you need more information.

1. _____

2. _____

3. _____

4. _____

5. _____

La ciudad es _____.

3. Which of the two cities would you rather visit and why? _____

_____

Nombre _____ Clase _____ Fecha _____

Communicative Activity 2-3B

1. Situation Your partner has found a postcard and information on a city. You'll be given five descriptions as clues to help you guess the city.

Task Take notes on the descriptions. Ask your partner in Spanish for help if you need more information.

MODELO A — Es una ciudad muy grande.

1. _muy grande_____

2. _____

3. _____

4. _____

5. _____

6. _____

La ciudad es _____.

2. Now you have a postcard of Paris. Give your partner five clues to help her or him guess what city it is. If your partner asks for extra clues, go ahead and provide them.

1. Nieva en el invierno.
2. Hay una torre muy famosa en el centro de la ciudad.
3. Está lejos de los Estados Unidos.
4. En esta ciudad está el museo de arte más famoso del mundo. (El Louvre)
5. La gente de esta ciudad habla francés.

3. Which of the two cities would you rather visit and why? _____

_____

Holt Spanish 2 ¡Ven conmigo!, Chapter 2

Communicative Activity 3-1 A

1. Situation You and your best friend are comparing your daily routines.

Task Ask your partner what a typical day is like for her or him by using the hints pictured in the chart below. Keep track of your partner's answers.

MODELO   A — De lunes a viernes, ¿te vistes con ropa cómoda?
          B — A veces me visto con ropa cómoda.

2. Now, check the box in the chart that best answers how often you do each of the following tasks: always, sometimes, or never.

De lunes a viernes

	siempre	a veces	nunca

3. Compare your chart with your partner's.

For which activities do you have the same routine? _____

_____

For which activities are your routines different? _____

_____

Communicative Activity 3-1 B

1. Situation You and your best friend are comparing your daily routines.

Task Check the box in the chart that best answers how often you do each of the tasks pictured below: always, sometimes, or never. Then, answer your partner's questions about what a typical day is like for you.

MODELO
A — **De lunes a viernes, ¿te vistes con ropa cómoda?**
B — **A veces me visto con ropa cómoda.**

De lunes a viernes

	siempre	a veces	nunca

2. Now, ask your partner what a typical day is like for her or him, using the hints pictured in the chart. Keep track of your partner's answers.

3. Compare your chart with your partner's.

For which activities do you have the same routine? _____

_____

For which activities are your routines different? _____

_____

Holt Spanish 2 ¡Ven conmigo!, Chapter 3

Communicative Activity 3-2A

1. **Situation** You and your partner are counselors at a summer camp. One of your responsibilities is to plan the schedule of chores a week in advance so that the campers don't repeat the same chore.

   Task You've spoken to Carmen, Joaquín, and Lisa. Your partner has spoken to Silvia, Alonso, and Luis. Find out who did each task on the list.

   MODELO   A — ¿Quién sacó la basura?
                     B — Luis la sacó.

   ### Quehaceres

1. Sacar la basura	**4.** Lavar los platos
2. Preparar las comidas	**5.** Reciclar
3. Quitar la mesa	**6.** Pasar la aspiradora

2. Now, use your list to answer your partner's questions about what chores Carmen, Joaquín, and Lisa did.

   QUEHACERES DE ESTA SEMANA

LUIS	*Sacó la basura.*
CARMEN	*Pasó la aspiradora.*
JOAQUÍN	*Recicló.*
LISA	*Lavó los platos.*
SILVIA	_____
ALONSO	_____

3. Now that you have all the information, plan next week's schedule with your partner.

Nombre _____ Clase _____ Fecha _____

 Communicative Activity 3-2B

COMMUNICATIVE ACTIVITIES

1. **Situation** You and your partner are counselors at a summer camp. One of your responsibilities is to plan the schedule of chores a week in advance so that the campers don't repeat the same chore.

Task You've spoken to Silvia, Alonso, and Luis. Your partner has spoken to Carmen, Joaquín, and Lisa. Use your list to answer your partner's question about what chores Silvia, Alonso, and Luis did.

MODELO   A — ¿Quién sacó la basura?
           B — Luis la sacó.

QUEHACERES DE ESTA SEMANA

LUIS   *Sacó la basura.*

CARMEN   _____

JOAQUÍN _____

LISA   _____

SILVIA   *Quitó la mesa.*

ALONSO   *Preparó las comidas.*

---

2. Now, find out who did each remaining chore on the list.

Quehaceres

1. Sacar la basura   4. Lavar los platos

2. Preparar las comidas 5. Reciclar

3. Quitar la mesa   6. Pasar la aspiradora

---

3. Now that you have all the information, plan next week's schedule with your partner.

16 Activities for Communication   Holt Spanish 2 ¡Ven conmigo!, Chapter 3

Copyright © by Holt, Rinehart and Winston. All rights reserved.

Communicative Activity 3-3A

1. **Situation** You and your partner are going to spend a month with the González family in Montevideo, Uruguay. Family members are Berta, Adrián, and their six children: Alberto, Lourdes, Fernando, Marisol, Manuel, and Isabel. You've decided to find out what the children's hobbies and pastimes are in order to bring them some gifts.

Task Your partner knows about Alberto, Lourdes, and Manuel's hobbies, and you know about the others. Find out what each child likes and dislikes.

MODELO   A — ¿Qué le gusta a ...?
                  B — Está loco/a ... También le interesa ... Pero no le gusta ...

Niño/a	Está loco/a por...	Le interesa(n...)	No le gusta(n)...
Alberto			
Lourdes			
Manuel			
Fernando	nadar y bucear	cocinar	los videojuegos
Marisol	leer y dibujar	los deportes	coleccionar nada
Isabel	acampar y pescar	patinar	tocar instrumentos

2. Now, answer your partner's questions about what Fernando, Marisol, and Isabel like and dislike.

3. Now that you both know what the children like, decide together what gifts you can bring them.

Niño/a	¿Qué regalo le compramos?
Alberto	
Lourdes	
Manuel	
Fernando	
Marisol	
Isabel	

COMMUNICATIVE ACTIVITIES

Communicative Activity 3-3B

1. **Situation** You and your partner are going to spend a month with the González family in Montevideo, Uruguay. Family members are Berta, Adrián, and their six children: Alberto, Lourdes, Fernando, Marisol, and Isabel. You've decided to find out what the children's hobbies and pastimes are in order to bring them some gifts.

    Task You know about Alberto, Lourdes, and Manuel's hobbies, and your partner knows about the others. Answer your partner's questions about their likes and dislikes.

    MODELO   A — ¿Qué le gusta a ...?
                   B — Está loco/a por ... También le interesa ... Pero no le gusta ...

Niño/a	Está loco/a por...	Le interesa(n...)	No le gusta(n)...
Alberto	las computadoras	los monopatines	nadar
Lourdes	la música	los videojuegos	reunirse con los amigos
Manuel	coleccionar estampillas	tocar en una banda	trabajar en mecánica
Fernando			
Marisol			
Isabel			

2. Now, find out what Fernando, Marisol, and Isabel like and dislike.

3. Now that you both know what the children like, decide together what gifts you can bring them.

Niño/a	¿Qué regalo le compramos?
Alberto	
Lourdes	
Manuel	
Fernando	
Marisol	
Isabel	

Communicative Activity 4-1A

1. Situation You're a peer counselor at your school, and your partner has come to you for advice on how to do better in a few classes.

Task Ask if your partner does the things listed below. Give advice based on the answers your partner gives.

MODELO
A — ¿Llegas a clase a tiempo todos los días?
B — A veces no llego a tiempo.
A — En el colegio, hay que llegar a tiempo todos los días.
B — Bien.

Para sacar buenas notas
1. llegar a clase a tiempo
2. prestar atención
3. tomar apuntes
4. hacer preguntas
5. seguir las instrucciones
6. entregar la tarea

2. Now, switch roles. Your partner is a peer counselor, and you've gone to see him or her for advice. Answer your partner's questions based on the information you put together from your teachers' comments in the checklist below. Then take notes based on the advice your partner gives.

	siempre	a veces no	nunca
1. dejar el libro en casa			✔
2. preocuparse	✔		
3. repasar los apuntes	✔		
4. entregar la tarea		✔	
5. hacer preguntas		✔	

3. Which of you needed more advice? _____

Communicative Activity 4-1 B

1. Situation Your partner is a peer counselor at your school, and you've gone to see him or her for advice on how to do better in a few classes. You've put together the following checklist of your teachers' comments.

Task As your partner asks you questions, answer using your checklist. Then take notes based on the advice your partner gives.

MODELO
A — ¿Llegas a clase a tiempo todos los días?
B — A veces no llego a tiempo.
A — En el colegio, hay que llegar a tiempo todos los días.
B — Bien.

	siempre	a veces no	nunca
1. llegar a clase a tiempo		✔	
2. tomar apuntes	✔		
3. seguir las instrucciones	✔		
4. prestar atención		✔	
5. entregar la tarea	✔		
6. hacer preguntas			✔

2. Now, switch roles. You're a peer counselor at your school, and your partner has come to you for advice. Ask if your partner does the things listed below. Give advice based on the answers your partner gives.

Para sacar buenas notas
1. repasar los apuntes
2. hacer preguntas
3. dejar el libro en casa
4. preocuparse
5. entregar la tarea

3. Which of you needed more advice? _____

Communicative Activity 4-2A

1. **Situation** You and your partner are conducting a psychology experiment about perception. Each of you will ask questions about pictures on the other's page.

Task Answer your partner's questions about each picture.

MODELO   B — ¿Cuál de las dos personas tiene la boca más grande?

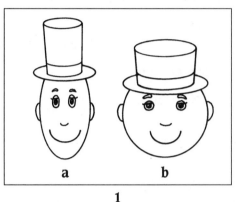

1

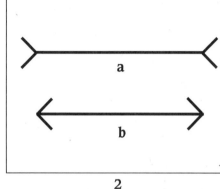

2

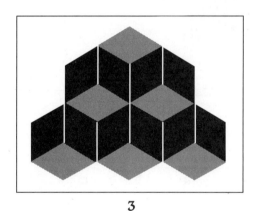

3

2. Now, ask the following questions and record your partner's response to each. Don't tell her or him the answers yet.

1. ¿Qué palabra es más brillante? _____ (Respuesta: **ninguna**)

2. ¿La línea **ab** es más corta que la línea **bc**? _____ (Respuesta: **no**)

3. ¿La caja **a** es más pequeña que la caja **c**? _____ (Respuesta: **no**)

3. Now, tell each other the correct answers. Who got more right, you or your partner?

_____

Nombre _____ Clase _____ Fecha _____

Communicative Activity 4-2B

1. **Situation** You and your partner are conducting a psychology experiment about perception. Each of you will ask questions about pictures on the other's page.

Task Ask your partner the following questions, and record her or his response. Don't tell her or him the correct answers yet.

MODELO   B — ¿Cuál de las dos personas tiene la boca más grande?

1. ¿Cuál de las dos personas tiene la boca más grande? _____ (Respuesta: **ninguna**)

2. ¿Qué línea es más larga? _____ (Respuesta: **ninguna**)

3. ¿Cuántos cubos ves? _____ (Respuesta: **tres o cinco**)

2. Now, answer your partner's questions about the following pictures.

1

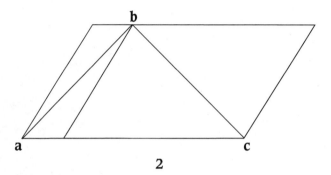

2

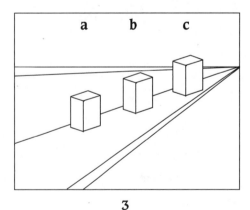

3

3. Now, tell each other the correct answers. Who got more right, you or your partner?

_____

Communicative Activity 4-3A

1. Situation You want to get together and do something with a friend you haven't seen for a while (your partner). The only trouble is that both of you are very busy these days.

Task You've found some free time during the week and have made a list of things you might like to do. Invite your friend to do the activities on the list. Don't stop until he or she accepts an invitation.

MODELO
    A — **Pienso ir al museo de antropología el miércoles. ¿Te gustaría ir conmigo?**

    B — **¿El miércoles? Lo siento, pero no puedo. Tengo que ir al cine con mis primos.**

    A — **¡Qué lástima! Si quieres, caminamos en el parque el martes.**

> ir al museo de antropología el miércoles
>
> caminar en el parque el martes
>
> ir al campo el sábado por la tarde
>
> ir a una fiesta el sábado
>
> ir al teatro el jueves por la noche
>
> ir al acuario el domingo

2. Now your friend is trying to invite you to do something during the week. Use your datebook to see whether or not you can go. If you can go, accept the invitation. If you can't, politely turn it down.

día y fecha	eventos y citas
domingo, 21 de marzo	visitar a mis abuelos
lunes, 22 de marzo	mucha tarea: composición de inglés
martes, 23 de marzo	tarea de química: leer el Capítulo 9
miércoles, 24 de marzo	partido de fútbol a las 6
jueves, 25 de marzo	ir al zoológico después de clases
viernes, 26 de marzo	mirar la televisión
sábado, 27 de marzo	el museo con Marián por la tarde

3. What did you end up doing together?

_____

_____

COMMUNICATIVE ACTIVITIES

Communicative Activity 4-3B

1. Situation You want to get together and do something with a friend you haven't seen for a while (your partner). The only trouble is that both of you are very busy these days.

Task Your friend is trying to invite you to do something during the week. Use your datebook to see whether or not you can go. If you can go, accept the invitation. If you can't, politely turn it down.

MODELO   A — **Pienso ir al museo de antropología el miércoles. ¿Te gustaría ir conmigo?**

                B — **¿El miércoles? Lo siento, pero no puedo. Tengo que ir al cine con mis primos.**

                A — **¡Qué lástima! Si quieres, caminamos en el parque el martes.**

día y fecha	eventos y citas
domingo, 21 de marzo	¡Qué día más aburrido!
lunes, 22 de marzo	biblioteca a las 7 con Marimar; geografía Capítulo 8
martes, 23 de marzo	piscina con Mariana a las 4; tarea de español
miércoles, 24 de marzo	ir al cine con mis primos
jueves, 25 de marzo	estudiar para el examen de química
viernes, 26 de marzo	examen de química; fiesta de José Luis a las 10
sábado, 27 de marzo	todo el día con los tíos

2. Now you've found some free time during the week and have made a list of things you might like to do. Invite your friend to do the activities on the list. Don't stop until he or she accepts an invitation.

> ir al parque de atracciones el lunes
>
> ir a comer en un restaurante el miércoles a las seis
>
> ir al cine el sábado por la tarde
>
> ir a una fiesta de cumpleaños el viernes a las nueve
>
> ir al lago a nadar el domingo por la tarde

3. What did you end up doing together?

_____

_____

Nombre _____ Clase _____ Fecha _____

1. Situation You and your partner are talking about things you do and have done to stay healthy and in shape.

Task Ask your partner what he or she regularly does to stay healthy. Be sure to get examples of what he or she did recently to stay healthy. Take notes on the answers he or she gives.

MODELO   A — ¿Qué haces para estar en plena forma?
           B — Asisto a una clase de ejercicios aeróbicos los
                lunes y miércoles.
                    or
           B — Ayer me moví por dos horas.

2. You've taken notes on some of the things you do and have done recently to stay in shape. Use the information from your notes below to answer your partner's questions.

	siempre	ayer
	✔	
	✔	
		✔
		✔
		✔

3. Now, compare your answers. Which one of you did more things recently to stay in shape? Which one of you does more things on a regular basis?

_____

_____

Holt Spanish 2 ¡Ven conmigo!, Chapter 5   Activities for Communication **25**

Communicative Activity 5-1 B

1. Situation You and your partner are talking about things you do and have done to stay healthy and in shape.

Task You've taken notes on some of the things you do and have done recently to stay in shape. Use the information from your notes below to answer your partner's questions.

MODELO   A —¿Qué haces para estar en plena forma?
B — Asisto a una clase de ejercicios aeróbicos los
lunes y miércoles.
    or
B — Ayer me moví por dos horas.

	siempre	ayer
	✔	
	✔	
	✔	
GIMNASIO Metamorfosis		✔
		✔

2. Now, ask your partner what he or she regularly does to stay healthy. Be sure to get examples of what he or she did recently to stay healthy. Take notes on the answers he or she gives.

3. Now, compare your answers. Which one of you did more things recently to stay in shape? Which one of you does more things on a regular basis?

_____

_____

Nombre _____ Clase _____ Fecha _____

Communicative Activity 5-2A

COMMUNICATIVE ACTIVITIES

1. Situation You're the coach at your school, and you've made a checklist of health-related activities. Now you're interviewing the athletes to find out if they need to change any habits.

Task Look at each item on your checklist. Tell the student athlete (your partner) *to do* each healthy activity and *not to do* the unhealthy ones. Put a check in the first column if she or he is already following your instructions, or in the second if a change needs to be made.

MODELO   A — **Evita la grasa.**
                  B — **Ya evito la grasa.** (or) **Está bien.**

Actividad	No necesita cambiar	Necesita cambiar
evitar la grasa		
levantar pesas		
no añadir sal a la comida		
correr todos los días		
hacer abdominales		
no salir todas las noches		

2. Now you are an athlete, and you've taken a personal inventory of the activities your coach is concerned about. As your coach tells you what to do or not to do, look at your chart. If you're already following the coach's instructions, say so. If you need to change your ways, say **Está bien.**

Actividad	Sí	No
pasear en bici	✔	
fumar	✔	
ir al gimnasio	✔	
comer muchas verduras verdes		✔
dormir demasiado		✔
poner mucha sal en la comida		✔

3. Compare checklists with your partner. Who do you think has the healthier lifestyle?

_____

Why? _____

Holt Spanish 2 ¡Ven conmigo!, Chapter 5   Activities for Communication   **27**

Communicative Activity 5-2B

1. Situation Your school's coach (your partner) has made a checklist of health-related activities. Now he or she is interviewing you to find out if you need to change any habits. You've taken a personal inventory of the activities your coach is concerned about.

Task As your coach tells you what to do or not to do, look at your chart. If you're already following the coach's instructions, say so. If you need to change your ways, say **Está bien**.

MODELO   A — **Evita la grasa.**
               B — **Ya evito la grasa.** (or) **Está bien.**

Actividad	Sí	No
correr todos los días	✔	
hacer abdominales	✔	
añadir sal a la comida	✔	
evitar la grasa		✔
levantar pesas		✔
salir todas las noches		✔

2. Now you are the coach. Look at each item on your checklist. Tell the student athlete (your partner) *to do* each healthy activity and *not to do* the unhealthy ones. Put a check in the first column if she or he is already following your instructions, or in the second if a change needs to be made.

Actividad	No necesita cambiar	Necesita cambiar
ir al gimnasio		
no fumar		
no dormir demasiado		
no poner mucha sal en la comida		
pasear en bici		
comer muchas verduras verdes		

3. Compare checklists with your partner. Who do you think has the healthier lifestyle?

_____

Why? _____

COMMUNICATIVE ACTIVITIES

1. **Situation** You missed seeing your best friend (your partner) all weekend. You call on Sunday evening to ask why you weren't able to get together.

Task Ask your friend about each of the following activities.

MODELO   A — ¿Por qué no jugaste al tenis después de las clases el viernes?
            B — Iba a jugar pero no pude. Es que me lastimé el codo.

DÍA Y FECHA	EVENTOS Y CITAS
viernes, 14 de octubre	jugar al tenis después de clases
	ir al concierto por la noche
sábado, 15 de octubre	asistir a una clase de ejercicios aeróbicos por la mañana
domingo, 16 de octubre	visitar el museo con Marián por la tarde

2. Now, switch roles. Explain to your friend why you weren't able to get together all weekend. Use one of these reasons in each of your explanations.

MODELO   B — ¿Por qué no fuiste al zoológico después de las clases el viernes?
            A — Iba a ir pero no pude. Es que mis padres no me dieron permiso.

(padres) no dar permiso

olvidarse

torcerse el tobillo

enfermarse

3. Now, look at both lists of activities. Which would you regret missing the most?

_____

Why? _____

Nombre _____ Clase _____ Fecha _____

 Communicative Activity 5-3B

1. Situation You missed seeing your best friend (your partner) all weekend. Since you had plans to spend time together, your friend calls on Sunday evening to see what happened.

Task Tell your friend the reasons you missed each of the weekend activities. Use one of these reasons in each of your explanations.

MODELO   A — ¿Por qué no jugaste al tenis después de las clases el viernes?
          B — Iba a jugar pero no pude. Es que me lastimé el codo.

| lastimarse el codo |
| perder las llaves del carro |
| dormir hasta muy tarde |
| estudiar para un examen |

2. Now, switch roles. Ask your friend why he or she was unable to do the following activities.

MODELO   B — ¿Por qué no fuiste al zoológico después de las clases el viernes?
          A — Iba a ir pero no pude. Es que mis padres no me dieron permiso.

DÍA Y FECHA	EVENTOS Y CITAS
viernes, 21 de octubre	ir al zoológico después de las clases
	reunirse con los amigos por la noche
sábado, 22 de octubre	participar en la competencia de ciclismo
domingo, 23 de octubre	levantarse temprano para ir al gimnasio

3. Now, look at both lists of activities. Which would you regret missing the most?

_____

Why? _____

Holt Spanish 2 ¡Ven conmigo!, Chapter 5

Communicative Activity 6-1 A

1. Situation You and your partner are trying to find an appropriate site for an international science fiction convention. You've each researched several cities, and now you need to pool your information. You've each made charts summarizing your research.

Task Ask your partner about the facilities in the cities on the chart. Take notes on the answers.

MODELO   A — ¿Sabe usted si hay un aeropuerto internacional en Los Ángeles?
               B — Sí, claro. Es muy grande.
               A — ¿Me podría decir dónde está el centro de convenciones?
               B — No estoy seguro/a. Lo siento.

ciudad	aeropuerto internacional	transporte público	centro de convenciones
Los Ángeles	✔		?
Nueva York			
Seattle			
Santa Fe			

2. Now, use the information below to answer your partner's questions about the cities you've researched. Where there's a question mark, say you're not sure.

ciudad	aeropuerto internacional	transporte público	centro de convenciones
Chicago	sí	metro, autobuses, taxis	centro de la ciudad
Houston	sí	autobuses, taxis	?
Memphis	?	autobuses, taxis	cerca del aeropuerto
Detroit	sí	?	centro de la ciudad

3. Now that you both have all the information, work together to decide which city should host the convention.

_____

Why? _____

Nombre _____ Clase _____ Fecha _____

 Communicative Activity 6-1 B

1. **Situation** You and your partner are trying to find an appropriate site for an international science fiction convention. You've each researched several cities, and now you need to pool your information. You've each made charts summarizing your research.

Task Use the chart below to answer your partner's questions about the cities you've researched. Where there's a question mark, say you're not sure.

MODELO A — ¿Sabe usted si hay un aeropuerto internacional en Los Ángeles?
B — Sí, claro. Es muy grande.
A — ¿Me podría decir dónde está el centro de convenciones?
B — No estoy seguro/a. Lo siento.

ciudad	aeropuerto internacional	transporte público	centro de convenciones
Los Ángeles	sí	metro, autobuses, taxis	?
Nueva York	sí	metro, autobuses, taxis	centro de la ciudad
Seattle	sí	?	cerca del aeropuerto
Santa Fe	?	autobuses, taxis	centro de la ciudad

2. Now, ask your partner about the facilities in the following cities. Take notes on the answers.

ciudad	aeropuerto internacional	transporte público	centro de convenciones
Chicago			
Houston			
Memphis			
Detroit			

3. Now that you both have all the information, work together to decide which city should host the convention.

_____

Why? _____

Holt Spanish 2 ¡Ven conmigo!, Chapter 6

Communicative Activity 6-2A

1. Situation Your partner is showing you a series of photos taken on a trip he or she recently went on.

Task Find out in what order your partner did the things in the photos by asking what he or she did first, afterwards, and so on. Number the photos as you go along.

MODELO A —¿Adónde fueron para empezar?
B — Para empezar, fuimos a la estación de tren.

P _____

E _____

R _____

U _____

T _____

2. Now you're telling your partner about a recent trip you went on. Below is a copy of your itinerary (list of things you did and in what order you did them). Answer your partner's questions about what you and your family members did and in what order. Then ask your partner to guess where you went.

Itinerario de nuestro viaje a París

____✔____ 1. Mi familia y yo / ir a la Torre Eiffel
____✔____ 2. Mi papá y mi hermano / comer en un café francés
____✔____ 3. Mi hermana / bajar el Río Seine en lancha
____✔____ 4. Mis hermanos y yo / sacar fotos de la Catedral Notre Dame
____✔____ 5. Mi familia y yo / visitar el Museo Louvre

3. Now, join the letters under each photo in the order the events took place. Put them together with your partner's to determine where your partner will go on his or her next vacation.

_____

COMMUNICATIVE ACTIVITIES

 Communicative Activity 6-2B

1. **Situation** You're telling your partner about a recent trip you went on. Below is a copy of your itinerary (list of things you did and in what order you did them).

Task Answer your partner's questions about what you and your family members did and in what order. Then ask your partner to guess where you went.

MODELO   A — ¿Adónde fueron para empezar?
         B — Para empezar, fuimos a la estación de tren.

Itinerario de nuestro viaje a Texas

✔	1.	Mamá y yo / ir a la Torre de las Américas
✔	2.	Mi familia y yo / comer en un café mexicano
✔	3.	Mi hermano / hacer un recorrido por el Jardín Botánico
✔	4.	Mi papá / sacar fotos del Álamo
✔	5.	Mi hermano y yo / visitar una misión española

2. Now your partner is showing you a series of photos taken on a trip he or she recently went on. Find out in what order your partner did the things in the photos by asking what he or she did first, afterwards, and so on. Number the photos as you go along. Then guess where your partner went.

O _____

C _____

I _____

O _____

R _____

3. Now, join the letters under each photo in the order the events took place. Put them together with your partner's to determine where your partner will go on his or her next vacation.

_____

_____

Holt Spanish 2 ¡Ven conmigo!, Chapter 6

Nombre _____ Clase _____ Fecha _____

Communicative Activity 6-3A

1. Situation You're a waiter or waitress at a Mexican food restaurant. You've taken notes to warn your customer about anything that might be wrong with today's food.

Task Take your partner's order. If he or she orders something that's not good today, explain why you don't recommend it.

MODELO
A — ¿Ya sabe usted qué va a pedir?
B — Sí. Para comenzar, la sopa de pollo, por favor.
A — No la recomiendo. La sopa de pollo está tibia hoy.
B — Gracias. Mejor me trae...
A — Está bien. ¿Algo más?

La comida de hoy	Lo que pide el/la cliente
Entremés—la sopa de pollo: tibia	
Plato principal—la carne guisada: bastante salada	
Postre—el helado: derretido	
Bebida—los refrescos: no muy fríos	

2. Now you're the customer. You've looked over the menu and narrowed your selection to the choices below for **un entremés, un plato principal, un postre,** and **una bebida.** Make a choice in each category and see if your waiter or waitress agrees with your selection.

RESTAURANTE
Rana Raúl

Entremés	*los nachos de frijoles y queso o las quesadillas*
Plato principal	*el plato vegetariano o los tacos de pollo*
Postre	*el flan de coco o sorbete de piña*
Bebida	*té, jugo de naranja o leche*

3. Compare lists with your partner. Then work together to name an item in each category that doesn't appear on either list.

_____

_____

Communicative Activity 6-3B

1. Situation You're a customer at a Mexican food restaurant. You've looked over the menu and narrowed your selection to the choices below for **un entremés, un plato principal, un postre,** and **una bebida.**

Task Make a choice in each category and see if your waiter or waitress agrees with your selection.

MODELO A — ¿Ya sabe usted qué va a pedir?
B — Sí. Para comenzar, la sopa de pollo, por favor.
A — No la recomiendo. La sopa de pollo está tibia hoy.
B — Gracias. Mejor me trae...
A — Está bien. ¿Algo más?

LA CASA DE CARLITOS

Entremés . . . . la sopa de pollo o una
ensalada de guacamole

Plato principal . . . los burritos (de res o de pollo)
o la carne guisada

Postre . . . . el helado de fresa o pan dulce

Bebida . . . . una limonada, un refresco
o café

2. Now you're the waiter or waitress. You've taken notes to warn your customer about anything that might be wrong with today's food. Take your partner's order. If he or she orders something that's not good today, explain why you don't recommend it.

La comida de hoy	Lo que pide el/la cliente
Entremés—las quesadillas: no muy calientes	
Plato principal—los tacos de pollo: bastante picantes	
Postre—el flan de coco: no sabroso	
Bebida—jugo de naranja: un poco agrio	

3. Compare lists with your partner. Then work together to name an item in each category that doesn't appear on either list.

_____

_____

Holt Spanish 2 ¡Ven conmigo!, Chapter 6

Nombre _____ Clase _____ Fecha _____

Communicative Activity 7-1 A

1. Situation You and your partner are writing an article for the yearbook about what some of your teachers used to do when they were teenagers. They've given you photos to go with the article.

Task Ask your partner what each of the following teachers used to do. Write each teacher's name under his or her photo.

MODELO   A — ¿Qué hacía el señor Reyes cuando era joven?
                  B — Pescaba con su hermanito.

señor Ruiz
señorita Quiñones
señor Santiago
señor Piñero
señora Ramos

señor Reyes

_____ _____ _____ _____ _____

2. Now, answer your partner's questions about each of these teachers.

señor Cancel   señorita Ortiz   señora Ocasio   señora Medrano   señorita Medina

3. Compare the photos with your partner.

Which teachers do you think were the most outgoing teenagers?

_____

Which were the most studious?

_____

Which were the most athletic?

_____

Nombre _____ Clase _____ Fecha _____

Communicative Activity 7-1 B

1. Situation You and your partner are writing an article for the yearbook about what some of your teachers used to do when they were teenagers. They've given you photos to go with the article.

Task Answer your partner's questions about what each teacher used to do according to the photos.

MODELO   A — ¿Qué hacía el señor Reyes cuando era joven?
                B — Pescaba con su hermanito.

señor Reyes

 señor Santiago   señor Ruiz   señora Ramos   señorita Quiñones   señor Piñero

2. Now, ask your partner about these teachers and write each teacher's name under his or her photo.

señorita Medina
señora Ocasio
señora Medrano
señorita Ortiz
señor Cancel

_____   _____   _____   _____   _____

3. Compare the photos with your partner.

Which teachers do you think were the most outgoing teenagers?

_____

Which were the most studious?

_____

Which were the most athletic?

_____

          Holt Spanish 2 ¡Ven conmigo!, Chapter 7

Communicative Activity 7-2A

1. Situation You're a police officer investigating a bank robbery that took place yesterday. One woman was seen fleeing the scene, and you've just picked up three suspects. Your partner was a witness and can describe what the robber looked like and what she was wearing.

Task Ask your partner what the woman looked like and what she was wearing. Based on what your partner tells you, decide which of the three women is the most likely suspect.

MODELO   A — ¿Cómo era ella?
            B — No era muy alta.

         a.   b.   c.

2. You saw a man fleeing the scene of a jewelry store heist yesterday. You wrote down some details so you could give an accurate description to the police. Use your notes to describe what the man looked like and what he was wearing.

> zapatos negros
> pelo corto
> camisa blanca con corbata
> de estatura mediana
> pantalones grises

3. Which suspect best matches the description? _____

Now, review the descriptions with your partner to find at least one detail that eliminated each of the other suspects.

_____

_____

Communicative Activity 7-2B

1. Situation You saw a woman fleeing the scene of a bank robbery yesterday. You wrote down some details so you could give an accurate description to the police (your partner).

Task Use your notes to answer your partner's questions about what the woman looked like and what she was wearing.

MODELO   A — ¿Cómo era ella?
               B — No era muy alta.

> *no muy alta*
> *rubia*
> *falda negra*
> *sandalias con calcetines blancos*
> *pelo largo*
> *camisa de rayas*

2. Now you're a police officer and you've just picked up three men suspected in a jewelry store heist that took place yesterday. Your partner was a witness who saw someone fleeing the scene. Ask your partner what the man looked like and what he was wearing. Based on what your partner tells you, decide which of the three men is the most likely suspect.

a.

b.

c.

3. Which suspect best matches the description? _____

Now, review the descriptions with your partner to find at least one detail that eliminated each of the other suspects.

_____

_____

Communicative Activity 7-3A

1. Situation You and your partner are conducting a survey to compare the habits of students in 1980 to the habits of students today. You did some historical research and turned up data on students in 1980. Your partner surveyed 100 students last week about their habits today.

Task Answer your partner's questions about what students used to do in 1980 using the information in the following chart.

MODELO B — ¿Cuántas horas al día pasaban los estudiantes en clases?
A — Pasaban siete horas al día en clases.

Análisis de costumbres estudiantiles

Actividad	1980	Hoy
pasar tiempo en clases	7 horas al día	
estudiar	1 hora al día	
ver televisión	5 horas a la semana	
pasar tiempo en actividades extracurriculares	media hora al día	
almorzar en restaurantes	1 día a la semana	
hacer ejercicio	8 horas a la semana	
leer el periódico	2 días a la semana	

2. Now, fill in the rest of your chart by asking your partner about students' habits today.

3. Together with your partner, discuss the data you've compiled. How do the students of 1980 compare to the students of today with regard to the following traits?

aplicado _____

flojo _____

responsable _____

trabajador _____

Communicative Activity 7-3B

1. Situation You and your partner are conducting a survey to compare the habits of students in 1980 to the habits of students today. Your partner did some historical research and turned up data on students in 1980. You surveyed 100 students last week about their habits today and compiled your own chart.

Task Fill in the following chart by asking your partner questions about what students used to do in 1980.

MODELO   B — ¿Cuántas horas al día pasaban los estudiantes en clases?
              A — Pasaban siete horas al día en clases.

Análisis de costumbres estudiantiles

Actividad	1980	Hoy
pasar tiempo en clases		7 horas al día
estudiar		3 horas al día
ver televisión		4 horas a la semana
pasar tiempo en actividades extracurriculares		una hora y media al día
almorzar en restaurantes		4 días a la semana
hacer ejercicio		5 horas a la semana
leer el periódico		4 días a la semana

2. Now, answer your partner's questions about students' habits today.

3. Together with your partner, discuss the data you've compiled. How do the students of 1980 compare to the students of today with regard to the following traits?

aplicado _____

flojo _____

responsable _____

trabajador _____

Nombre _____ Clase _____ Fecha _____

1. **Situation** You and your partner are investigating possible sites for a year-end field trip for your class. You went to an amusement park this weekend, and your partner went to the zoo.

Task You're interested in knowing about the following animals at the zoo: *the tigers, the turtles, the parrots,* and *the snakes.* First, ask your partner what kind of time he or she had at the zoo and then ask specifically about the animals. Take notes.

MODELO   A — ¿Qué tal lo pasaste en el zoológico?
               B — Lo pasé bien.
               A — ¿Qué tal estuvieron los tigres?
               B — Estuvieron más o menos bien.

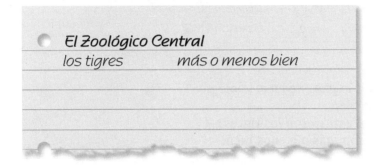

El Zoológico Central

los tigres	más o menos bien

2. Now, answer your partner's questions about what kind of time you had at the amusement park using the following notes you took.

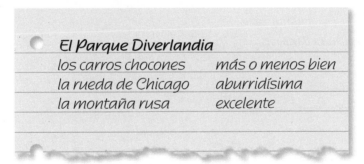

El Parque Diverlandia

los carros chocones	más o menos bien
la rueda de Chicago	aburridísima
la montaña rusa	excelente

3. Now, based on your conversation, decide which place you'd like to suggest the class go at the end of the year. Why?

_____

_____

_____

Communicative Activity 8-1 B

1. **Situation** You and your partner are scoping out possible sites for a year-end field trip for your class. You went to the zoo this weekend and your partner went to an amusement park.

Task Answer your partner's questions about what kind of time you had at the zoo using the following notes you took.

El Zoológico Central

los tigres	más o menos bien
las serpientes	de película
los loros y las tortugas	aburridísimos
los cocodrilos	buenísimos

MODELO   A — ¿Qué tal lo pasaste en el zoológico?
B — Lo pasé bien.
A — ¿Qué tal estuvieron los tigres?
B — Estuvieron más o menos bien.

2. Now you're interested in knowing about the following rides at the amusement park: *the bumper cars, the roller coaster,* and *the Ferris wheel.* Ask your partner what kind of time he or she had at the amusement park and then ask specifically about the rides. Take notes.

El Parque Diverlandia

3. Now, based on your conversation, decide which place you'd like to suggest the class go at the end of the year. Why?

_____

_____

_____

1. **Situation** You threw a party yesterday and invited all your friends. You were very disappointed when several people, including your partner, didn't show up and didn't let you know they weren't coming.

Task Starting with your partner, ask if he or she knows why the following people didn't come.

MODELO   A — ¿Por qué no asististe a la fiesta anoche?
            B — Quería ir pero no pude. Tenía que...

Tú
Mark
Linda
Ramón y Sergio
Clara

2. Your partner also had a party a few weeks ago, but something came up and you couldn't go. When you called some of your friends to ask how the party went, you found out that many of them couldn't go either. They all said that when they tried to let your partner know, the phone was busy.

Mi familia y yo

Tony y Chato

Cindy

Levanuel

Carmen

3. Discuss with your partner who of all the invitees had the best reason for not attending the party.

_____

_____

Communicative Activity 8-2B

1. Situation Your partner had a party yesterday, but something came up and you couldn't go. When you called some of your friends to ask how the party went, you found out that many of them couldn't go either. They all said that when they tried to let your partner know, the phone was busy.

Task As your partner asks about the people he or she missed at the party, explain what each had to do.

MODELO   A — ¿Por qué no asististe a la fiesta anoche?
                B — Quería ir pero no pude. Tenía que...

Mi familia y yo

Clara

Mark

Ramón y Sergio

Linda

2. A few weeks ago, the same thing happened at your party. Several friends you invited, including your partner, didn't show up and didn't let you know they weren't coming. Starting with your partner, ask if he or she knows why the following people didn't come.

Tú
Carmen
Levanuel
Tony y Chato
Cindy

3. Discuss with your partner who of all the invitees had the best reason for not attending the party.

_____

_____

Communicative Activity 8-3A

1. **Situation** You're a prosecutor looking for good witnesses to testify against three men suspected of robbing a bank. A good witness would give mostly first-hand information. A poor witness would mostly repeat hearsay, which can't be used as evidence in a trial.

Task Your partner was present during the holdup. Ask each question, then listen carefully as he or she answers. Mark the first column if the answer is first-hand information. Mark the second if it is only hearsay, indicated by **...me dijo/dijeron que...**

MODELO   A — ¿Cuántos hombres había?
          B — Había tres hombres.

	Información directa	Información indirecta
¿Cuántos hombres había?	✓	
¿Cómo entraron?		
¿Qué llevaban?		
¿Cómo eran?		
¿Tenían pistolas?		
¿Quiénes eran?		

2. Now you're making a statement about two women suspected of being pickpockets during a parade you attended. Use the chart below to answer each of your partner's questions. If you saw something, state it as a fact. If you heard it from someone else, say who gave you the information, using **...me dijo/dijeron que...** Feel free to embellish your story with descriptive detail.

¿Quién lo dijo?

Lo vi.	Había dos mujeres en el desfile.
Lo vi.	Llevaban disfraces.
un hombre	Una era gorda. La otro era delgada.
mi amiga Graciela	Pasaban entre la gente.
unos niños	Tenían muchas carteras.

3. Work with your partner to decide if each witness should testify in court. Justify your decisions.

Testigo 1: ¿Debe hablar en corte? _____ ¿Por qué sí o por qué no?

_____

_____

Testigo 2: ¿Debe hablar en corte? _____ ¿Por qué sí o por qué no?

_____

_____

Communicative Activity 8-3B

1. Situation You were present during a recent bank robbery, and now you're answering some questions about the crime. Your partner is a prosecutor trying to decide if you would make a good witness for the case. A good witness would give mostly first-hand information. A poor witness would mostly repeat hearsay, which can't be used as evidence in a trial.

Task Use the chart below to answer your partner's questions. If you saw something take place, state it as a fact. If you heard it from someone else, say who gave you the information, using **...me dijo/dijeron que...** Feel free to embellish your story with descriptive detail.

MODELO   A — ¿Cuántos hombres había?
           B — Había tres hombres.

¿Quién lo dijo?

Lo vi.	Había tres hombres.
Lo vi.	Entraron en el banco normalmente.
Lo vi.	Llevaban máscaras.
Lo vi.	Dos eran altos. Uno era bajo.
un hombre	Tenían pistolas.
unas amigas	Uno trabajaba en el banco.

2. Now you're a prosecutor looking for witnesses to testify against two women suspected of being pickpockets at a parade. Ask each question, then listen carefully as your partner answers. Mark the first column if the answer to each question is first-hand information. Mark the second if it is only hearsay.

	Información directa	Información indirecta
¿Cuántas mujeres había?		
¿Qué llevaban?		
¿Cómo eran?		
¿Qué hacían?		
¿Tenían carteras?		

3. Work with your partner to decide if each witness should testify in court. Justify your decisions.

Testigo 1: ¿Debe hablar en corte? _____ ¿Por qué sí o por qué no?

_____

Testigo 2: ¿Debe hablar en corte? _____ ¿Por qué sí o por qué no?

_____

Holt Spanish 2 ¡Ven conmigo!, Chapter 8

Communicative Activity 9-1A

1. Situation You work in the tourist office in your town. Your partner is a tourist who has come to your office to ask how to get to certain places.

Task Give the tourist directions to the places he or she asks about.

MODELO   B — Disculpe, ¿cómo se va al Museo de Arte?
               A — De aquí, hay que ir al este. El Museo de Arte queda entre la
                      Avenida de la Gran Cultura y la Avenida Pedernal.
               B — Muchas gracias.

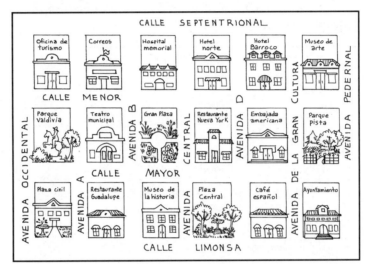

2. Now, switch roles. Ask for directions from the **Oficina de Turismo** to the **Plaza Central**, then to **Restaurante Nueva York**, from there to the **Ayuntamiento**, and finally to the **Plaza Civil**. Trace your route on the map as you go.

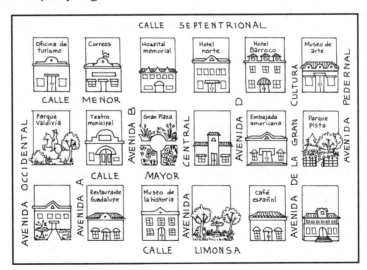

3. Now, compare the routes both you and your partner took while sightseeing. Which of you traveled the farthest?

Communicative Activity 9-1 B

1. Situation Your partner is an employee at the tourist office in the town you're visiting. You're a tourist who has stopped in at the Tourist Office to ask for directions to certain places.

Task Ask for directions from the **Oficina de Turismo** to the **Museo de Arte**, then to the **Restaurante Guadalupe**, from there to the **Gran Plaza**, and finally to the **Hotel Barroco**. Trace your route on your map as you go.

MODELO
    B — Disculpe, ¿cómo se va al Museo de Arte?
    A — De aquí, hay que ir al este. El Museo de Arte queda entre la
           Avenida de la Gran Cultura y la Avenida Pedernal.
    B — Muchas gracias.

2. Now, switch roles. You're the employee at the tourist office giving directions to the tourist. Answer each of the tourist's questions.

3. Now, compare the routes both you and your partner took while sightseeing. Which of you traveled the farthest?

Communicative Activity 9-2A

1. **Situation** You're the costume designer for the school play, and several cast members have come down with the flu and must be replaced by their understudies. Since the costumes were tailored for the original actors, you've asked the director to have the understudies try on their costumes and let you know which ones fit and which may need alterations.

Task Ask the director how each article of clothing in question fits the understudy. If the item fits well, put a check in the first column. If the costume has something wrong with it, write the problem in the second column.

MODELO   A — ¿Cómo le quedan los pantalones a Ricardo?
   B — Le quedan un poco anchos.

	Está bien	Hay un problema
Ricardo—los pantalones		un poco anchos
Inés—la falda		
Simón—las botas		
Soledad—el vestido		
Mingo—el traje		
Cristina—la blusa		

2. Now you're the director, and the costume designer wants to know which costumes fit and which will need alterations. Use your notes to answer your partner's questions about how everyone looks.

> Patricio—el suéter, estrecho
> Sergio—los pantalones cortos, muy anchos
> Gastón—las sandalias, muy grandes
> Mimi—se ve muy guapa
> Raquel—los bluejeans, muy de moda

3. Work with your partner to determine which articles of clothing may need to be replaced rather than merely altered.

_____

_____

Nombre _____ Clase _____ Fecha _____

COMMUNICATIVE ACTIVITIES

Communicative Activity 9-2B

1. Situation You're directing the school play, and several cast members have come down with the flu and must be replaced by their understudies. The costume designer wants to know which costumes fit the understudies and which may need alterations. The actors tried on their costumes, and you took notes on how they fit.

Task Use your notes to answer your partner's questions about how everyone looks.

MODELO   A — ¿Cómo le quedan los pantalones a Ricardo?
          B — Le quedan un poco anchos.

> Simón—las botas, estrechas
> Mingo—se ve guapo
> Cristina—la blusa no hace juego con la chaqueta
> Ricardo—los pantalones, un poco anchos
> Inés—se ve guapísima
> Soledad—el vestido, muy largo

2. Now you're the costume designer. Ask the director how each article of clothing in question fits the understudy. If the item fits well, put a check in the first column. If the costume has something wrong with it, write the problem in the second column.

	Está bien	Hay un problema
Sergio—los pantalones cortos		
Raquel—los bluejeans		
Mimi—el vestido		
Patricio—el suéter		
Gastón—las sandalias		

3. Work with your partner to determine which articles of clothing may need to be replaced rather than merely altered.

_____

_____

52 Activities for Communication

Holt Spanish 2 ¡Ven conmigo!, Chapter 9

Copyright © by Holt, Rinehart and Winston. All rights reserved.

Nombre _____ Clase _____ Fecha _____

1. **Situation** You're a merchant in an open-air market. Your goal is to make at least $75 on all the items you have for sale. Your partner is a potential customer. Each item has two prices; the first is your asking price and the second is the lowest acceptable price.

   Task You must sell each item, but not for less than its lowest acceptable price. Get as much money as you can for each item. Start by approaching your partner and asking him or her if you can be of service.

   MODELO   A — **Buenos días. ¿En qué le puedo servir?**
                    B — **Buenos días. Me gusta este suéter. ¿Cuánto es?**

joyero $7.00, $4.95

suéter
$24.50, $17.50

pulsera $12.50, $8.95

muñeca
$4.00,
$2.95

camisa $42.00, $29.00

2. Now, switch roles. You're shopping for gifts at an open-air market, and your partner is the merchant. You only have $200 to spend, and your goal is to buy all the items shown and still have about $10 left over for lunch. Ask the price of each item. If it's too high, bargain with the merchant and convince him or her to lower it. Keep track of how much you're spending and budget accordingly.

Sombrero.
Una ganga

En barata.

Piel artificial.
Oferta especial

Regalada

En descuento

3. Which of you made more money in the role of the merchant? _____

   Which of you got more bargains as the customer? _____

Holt Spanish 2 ¡Ven conmigo!, Chapter 9   Activities for Communication **53**

Nombre _____ Clase _____ Fecha _____

Communicative Activity 9-3B

1. Situation You're shopping for gifts at an open-air market, and your partner is the merchant. You only have $85 to spend, and your goal is to buy all the items shown and still have about $10 left over for lunch.

Task Ask the price of each item. If it's too high, bargain with the merchant and convince him or her to lower it. Keep track of how much you're spending and budget accordingly.

MODELO   A — **Buenos días. ¿En qué le puedo servir?**
              B — **Buenos días. Me gusta este suéter. ¿Cuánto es?**

2. Now, switch roles. You're a merchant in an open-air market. Your goal is to make at least $160 on all the items you have for sale. Your partner is a potential customer. Each item has two prices; the first is your asking price and the second is the lowest acceptable price. You must sell each item but not for less than its lowest acceptable price. Get as much money as you can for each item. Start by approaching your partner and asking him or her if you can be of service.

3. Which of you made more money in the role of the merchant? _____

Which of you got more bargains as the customer? _____

1. **Situation** Jaime and Esmerelda were married last weekend. Esmerelda wrote to you, and Jaime wrote to your partner about some of the things that happened during the weekend. They included some pictures with each letter. Their letters say that you can tell by the pictures what things were like when certain things happened. Unfortunately, Esmerelda sent you Jaime's pictures by mistake, and your partner has Esmerelda's pictures. Now, you want to find out what Esmerelda meant in her letter.

Task Ask your partner about each sentence of Esmerelda's letter. Your partner will answer according to the pictures he or she got by mistake. Take notes on the answers.

MODELO   A — ¿Cómo se sentían todos cuando se casaron Jaime y Esmerelda?
                  B — Todos se sentían muy felices.

Esmerelda's letter says:

Está claro en la foto cómo se sentían todos cuando nos casamos.

_____

Puedes ver cómo estaba el coche cuando nos fuimos.

_____

Mira qué tiempo hacía cuando se ponchó la llanta. ¡Qué horror!

_____

2. Now, answer your partner's questions about the circumstances of the events in the following pictures, which you got by mistake.

3. Which event from the wedding or honeymoon took place under the most bizarre circumstances?

_____

Nombre _____ Clase _____ Fecha _____

Communicative Activity 10-1 B

1. Situation Jaime and Esmerelda were married last weekend. Jaime wrote to you, and Esmerelda wrote to your partner about some of the things that happened during the weekend. They included some pictures with each letter. Their letters say that you can tell by the picture what things were like when certain things happened. Unfortunately, Jaime sent you Esmerelda's pictures by mistake, and your partner has Jaime's pictures.

Task Answer your partner's questions about the circumstances of the events in the following pictures, which you got by mistake.

MODELO   A — ¿Cómo se sentían todos cuando se casaron Jaime y Esmerelda?
             B — Todos se sentían muy felices.

2. Now, you want to find out what Jaime meant in his letter. Ask your partner about each sentence of Jaime's letter. Your partner will answer according to the pictures he or she has. Take notes on the answers.

Jaime's letter says:

Está claro qué tiempo hacía cuando nos perdimos en el bosque.

Ves en la foto cómo nos sentíamos cuando llamamos a la puerta.

Y mira qué ropa llevaba la gente que nos invitó a bailar.

3. Which event from the wedding or honeymoon took place under the most bizarre circumstances?

Communicative Activity 10-2A

1. **Situation** You and a group of friends just had a close encounter with a UFO. Below is a series of pictures showing your recollection of the event. A news reporter (your partner) is interviewing you about what happened.

Task The reporter wants to know what was happening before the space ship arrived, what happened when it did arrive, and how everything ended. Use the pictures to answer his or her questions.

MODELO B — ¿Qué hacían tú y tus amigos?
A — Mis amigos y yo caminábamos y hablábamos.

2. Now, switch roles. You're a reporter and it's your job to get the story from the group who had the encounter. You've prepared a list of questions. Be sure to take notes on the answers.

¿Qué hacían tú y tus amigos?
¿Qué tiempo hacía?
¿Qué hora era?
¿Dónde estaban?
Entonces ¿qué pasó?
¿Cómo era el OVNI?
¿Cómo eran los extraterrestres?
¿Qué pasó al final?

3. Compare your notes on the interviews. How do the two stories differ?

_____

_____

Communicative Activity 10-2B

1. Situation You're a news reporter interviewing a group of people who just had a close encounter with a UFO.

Task You've prepared a list of questions to ask one of the group members (your partner) about what was happening before the space ship arrived, what happened when it did arrive, and how everything ended. Be sure to take notes on the answers.

MODELO   B — ¿Qué hacían tú y tus amigos?
           A — Mis amigos y yo caminábamos y hablábamos.

¿Qué hacían tú y tus amigos?
¿Qué tiempo hacía?
¿Qué hora era?
¿Dónde estaban?
Entonces ¿qué pasó?
¿Cómo era el OVNI?
¿Cómo eran los extraterrestres?
¿Qué pasó al final?

2. Now, switch roles. You and your friends just encountered a UFO. Your partner (a news reporter) is asking questions about the event. Use the pictures below to answer his or her questions.

3. Compare your notes on the interviews. How do the two stories differ?

_____

_____

Holt Spanish 2 ¡Ven conmigo!, Chapter 10

Communicative Activity 10-3A

1. **Situation** You write for *El metiche*, a regional tabloid. You have a list of story ideas, and you want to find out if people would buy your paper if these were the lead stories.

Task Complete the following headlines appropriately, then read them to your partner. Based on his or her reaction, decide whether each idea would make a good cover story and mark the appropriate column.

MODELO   A — ¡El actor famoso Felipe Chulo se casa con una extraterrestre!
             B — ¡Qué va!

	Sí	No
El actor famoso *(actor's name)* se casa con una extraterrestre.		✔
¡La Torre de las Américas en San Antonio es una nave espacial!		
¡Niño se cae en un pozo!		
¡Extraterrestres con *(number)* brazos y *(number)* cabezas juegan al *(sport)*!		
¡Estudiantes ven un OVNI en *(your town)*!		
¡Se enamoran y se casan _____ y _____ en boda secreta!		

2. Now switch roles. Your partner works for *El chismoso* and wants to see how you react to some story ideas. Listen as your partner reads each headline, then if you would like to read the article, say something enthusiastic like **Cuéntamelo todo** or **¿De veras?** If you think the story sounds boring or silly, say something like **¡Qué va!** or **No lo puedo creer**.

3. With your partner, choose one of the headlines and write a brief news article about it.

_____

_____

_____

_____

_____

_____

_____

_____

_____

_____

_____

_____

Communicative Activity 10-3B

1. **Situation** A reporter from the regional tabloid *El metiche* wants to make sure his or her head-lines will sell papers. He or she is polling people to see how they respond to different story ideas.

Task React to the headlines as your partner reads them. If you would like to read the article, say something enthusiastic like **Cuéntamelo todo** or **¿De veras?** If you think the story sounds boring or silly, say something like **¡Qué va!** or **No lo puedo creer**.

MODELO   A — ¡El actor famoso Felipe Chulo se casa con una extraterrestre!
                   B — ¡Qué va!

2. Now you write for *El chismoso*, a regional tabloid. You have a list of story ideas, and you want to find out if people would buy your paper if these were the headlines. Complete the headlines appro-priately, then read them to your partner. Based on his or her reaction, decide whether each idea would make a good cover story and mark the appropriate column.

	Sí	No
¡Familia de monos cuida a un niño humano! Ahora puede hablar con los animales.		
¡Ladrones de otra galaxia roban todas las pizzerías—gran pánico en el colegio de *(your school)*!		
¡*(Famous singer or athlete)* dice que extraterrestres lo/la dejaron aquí cuando visitaron nuestro planeta!		
¡*(Famous deceased celebrity)* todavía vive! Tiene casa en *(your town)*.		
¡_____ rompe con _____! *(names of famous couple)*		

3. With your partner, choose one of the headlines and write a brief news article about it.

_____

_____

_____

_____

_____

_____

_____

_____

_____

_____

_____

Nombre _____ Clase _____ Fecha _____

Communicative Activity 11-1A

1. Situation You and your partner are surveying some of your friends as part of your science report on environmental problems.

Task Use the drawings below to ask your partner for the results of his or her survey. Write the number of people your partner answers with in the second column.

MODELO   A — ¿Cuántas personas creen que hay demasiado ruido en la ciudad?
              B — Catorce personas dicen que se preocupan por el ruido.

Problemas	Número de personas que responden que sí	Problemas	Número de personas que responden que sí	Problemas	Número de personas que responden que sí
	14				

2. Now, answer your partner's questions about the results of your survey.

MODELO   B — ¿Y cuántas personas dicen que hay mucha contaminación del lago?
              A — Nadie piensa en la contaminación del lago.

Problemas	Número de personas que responden que sí	Problemas	Número de personas que responden que sí	Problemas	Número de personas que responden que sí
	5		8		0
	0		12		

3. Según los estudiantes, ¿cuál es el problema más grande? _____

Nombre _____ Clase _____ Fecha _____

 Communicative Activity 11-1B

1. Situation You and your partner are surveying some of your friends as part of your science report on environmental problems.

Task Use the chart below to answer your partner's questions about the results of your survey.

MODELO A — ¿Cuántas personas creen que hay demasiado ruido en la ciudad?
B — Catorce personas dicen que se preocupan por el ruido.

Problemas	Número de personas que responden que sí	Problemas	Número de personas que responden que sí	Problemas	Número de personas que responden que sí
	14		8		16
	10		2		

2. Now, use the drawings below to ask your partner for the results of his or her survey. Write the number of people your partner answers with in the second column.

Problemas	Número de personas que responden que sí	Problemas	Número de personas que responden que sí	Problemas	Número de personas que responden que sí

3. Según los estudiantes, ¿cuál es el problema más grande? _____

62 Activities for Communication

Holt Spanish 2 ¡Ven conmigo!, Chapter 11

COMMUNICATIVE ACTIVITIES

Communicative Activity 11-2A

1. Situation You're writing an article for your school newspaper about environmental problems and consequences. Your partner has done some surveys to find out what five people's opinions are on the various issues and can give you a general idea of the student body's opinion.

Task Read your ideas for the article to your partner. Your partner will tell you whether or not the sampling of the student body agrees or disagrees. Tally the opinions in the appropriate column.

MODELO   A — **Hay muchas especies en peligro de extinción, por lo tanto es urgente hacer algo.**
          B — **Uno dijo "Así es la cosa." Otro dijo "¡Eso es!" Otro "Sin duda." Uno "Hasta cierto punto, pero..." Y alguien dijo "No sé."**

Tema	Opiniones		
	De acuerdo	En contra	Indeciso
Hay muchas especies en peligro de extinción, por lo tanto es urgente hacer algo.	✔✔✔		✔✔
Cada vez hay menos espacio en la Tierra.			
Hay demasiados automóviles y por consiguiente hay mucha contaminación.			
Desperdiciamos los recursos naturales.			
Tenemos que cuidar mejor las selvas tropicales.			

2. Now, switch roles. As your partner reads his or her ideas for the article, tell him or her how people responded in your survey.

Tema	Opiniones
El águila calva está en peligro de extinción.	No tienes razón.; No lo creo.; No me parece.; ¡Te equivocas!; No estoy segura.
La pobreza en Perú causa la pesca del delfín. Es urgente hacer algo contra la pobreza.	Así es la cosa.; Claro que sí.; Sin duda.; Tienes razón.; Estoy de acuerdo.
Vamos a enfrentar una crisis si no nos preparamos para la llegada de los extraterrestres.	¡Qué va!; ¡Te equivocas!; No me parece.; No lo creo.; Mira... no hay extraterrestres.
Hay demasiado ruido en las ciudades.	¡Qué va!; ¡Te equivocas!; No sé.; No lo creo.; Hasta cierto punto.

3. Based on the what you've learned, which topic do most students agree with? Which do most students disagree with?

_____

Nombre _____ Clase _____ Fecha _____

Communicative Activity 11-2B

1. Situation Your partner is writing an article for your school newspaper about environmental problems and consequences. To help out, you've surveyed five people to find out what their opinions are on the various issues and have recorded what they said in the chart below.

Task As your partner reads his or her ideas for the article, tell him or her how people responded in your survey.

MODELO   A — Hay muchas especies en peligro de extinción, por lo tanto es urgente hacer algo.

           B — Uno dijo "Así es la cosa." Otro dijo "¡Eso es!" Otro "Sin duda." Uno "Hasta cierto punto, pero..." Y alguien dijo "No sé."

Tema	Opiniones
Hay muchas especies en peligro de extinción, por lo tanto es urgente hacer algo.	Así es la cosa.; ¡Eso es!; Sin duda.; Hasta cierto punto, pero...; No sé.
Cada vez hay menos espacio en la Tierra.	No me parece.; ¡Te equivocas!; No lo creo.; Hasta cierto punto...; Estoy de acuerdo.
Hay demasiados automóviles y por consiguiente hay mucha contaminación.	¡Qué va!; Sí, tienes razón.; Estoy de acuerdo.; No me parece.; Así es la cosa.
Desperdiciamos los recursos naturales.	Así es la cosa.; ¡Claro que sí!; Sin duda.; Tienes razón.; ¡Eso es!
Tenemos que cuidar mejor las selvas tropicales.	Hasta cierto punto...; Así es la cosa.; Tienes razón.; Estoy de acuerdo.; ¡Te equivocas!

2. Now, switch roles. You're writing an article and your partner has information on five people's opinions about the following ideas. Read your ideas for the article to your partner. Your partner will tell you whether or not the sampling of the student body agrees or disagrees. Tally the opinions in the appropriate column.

Tema	Opiniones		
	De acuerdo	En contra	Indeciso
El águila calva está en peligro de extinción.			
La pobreza en Perú causa la pesca del delfín. Es urgente hacer algo para eliminar la pobreza.			
Vamos a enfrentar una crisis si no nos preparamos para la llegada de los extraterrestres.			
Hay demasiado ruido en las ciudades.			

3. Based on the what you've learned, which topic do most students agree with? Which do most students disagree with?

_____

Communicative Activity 11-3A

1. **Situation** You and your partner offered to put up copies of some posters that the ecology club made. After dividing up the posters, however, your partner realized that some of his or her posters were missing captions.

Task Read the captions slowly to your partner so he or she can write them on the incomplete posters. You may need to read the captions more than once.

MODELO   A — **Es necesario conservar energía.**
          B — **Repite, por favor.**

**Es necesario conser-
var energía**

**Todos deberíamos
evitar los productos
empacados.**

**Tú puedes reciclar
las latas.**

**Hay que proteger
las selvas tropi-
cales. Piensa en los
efectos sobre el
medio ambiente.**

2. Now, as your partner reads each caption, write it under the appropriate poster.

_____   _____   _____

_____   _____   _____

_____   _____   _____

_____   _____   _____

3. Discuss the posters with your partner. Which poster would be most helpful for your community and why?

_____

_____

Communicative Activity 11-3B

1. Situation You and your partner offered to put up copies of some posters that the ecology club made. After dividing up the posters, however, you realized that some of your posters were missing captions.

Task As your partner reads each caption, write it under the appropriate poster.

MODELO   A — **Es necesario conservar energía.**
           B — **Repite, por favor.**

Es necesario conser- _____ _____ _____

var energía. _____ _____ _____

_____ _____ _____ _____

_____ _____ _____ _____

2. Now, read the captions below slowly to your partner so he or she can write them on the incomplete posters. You may need to read the captions more than once.

Todos compartimos la Tierra. Hay que proteger las especies.

A todos nos toca mantener limpia nuestra ciudad.

Si cambiamos nuestro estilo de vida, podemos resolver los problemas.

3. Discuss the posters with your partner. Which poster would be most helpful for your community and why?

_____

_____

Communicative Activity 12-1A

1. **Situation** You and your partner are showing each other pictures of your vacations from last summer. You've each labeled the pictures in the photo album with dates and some other information about things that happened.

   Task Find out from your partner where he or she went last summer. Be sure to also ask what he or she did there and when.

   MODELO   A — ¿Adónde fuiste el verano pasado?
                   B — Fui a...
                   A — ¿Qué hiciste allí?
                   B — Bueno, el viernes...

2. Now, answer your partner's questions about where you went and what you did last summer. Be sure to tell when you did each thing based on the captions you wrote for each picture.

La Torre de las Américas

El viernes

El sábado

El domingo; con mi tío

El domingo; con mis parientes

3. Whose vacation lasted longer? _____

COMMUNICATIVE ACTIVITIES

Communicative Activity 12-1B

1. **Situation** You and your partner are showing each other pictures of your vacations from last summer. You've each labeled the pictures in the photo album with dates and some other information about things that happened.

Task Answer your partner's questions about where you went and what you did last summer. Be sure to tell when you did each thing based on the captions you wrote for each picture.

MODELO   A — ¿Adónde fuiste el verano pasado?
            B — Fui a...
            A — ¿Qué hiciste allí?
            B — Bueno, el viernes...

Mis parientes y yo en la Torre Eiffel

El lunes; el museo Louvre

Yo y mi nueva amiga en Notre Dame; el domingo

El martes

El jueves

2. Now, find out from your partner where he or she went last summer. Be sure to also ask what he or she did there and when.

3. Whose vacation lasted longer? _____

Nombre _____ Clase _____ Fecha _____

1. Situation Your partner has exciting plans for a trip this summer and wants you to guess where he or she is going. Your partner has given you five pictures from travel brochures. One of these shows his or her destination.

Task Use the cues below to ask questions about where your partner plans to go. Take notes and ask for any additional information you may need. When you're ready to guess, write the picture's letter in the blank.

MODELO   A — ¿Está rodeado de montañas?
                 B — No, no está rodeado de montañas.

a   b   c   d   e

rodeado de montañas	playa	clima	ciudad grande o pueblo pequeño	colinas	¿?
no					

El destino de mi compañero/a: _____

2. Now your partner is trying to guess where you're going this summer. Answer his or her questions based on the picture of your destination.

3. Show your partner the picture you chose. Did you guess correctly? _____

Look over all the pictures with your partner. Where would each of you really like to travel, and why?

_____

_____

_____

Holt Spanish 2 ¡Ven conmigo!, Chapter 12   Activities for Communication **69**

Communicative Activity 12-2B

1. **Situation** You have exciting plans for a trip this summer, and you want your partner to guess where you're going. You've given him or her five pictures from travel brochures. One of these shows your destination.

Task Based on the picture of your destination, answer your partner's questions about where you plan to go.

MODELO   A — ¿Está rodeado de montañas?

              B — No, no está rodeado de montañas.

2. Now, guess which of these five pictures shows where your partner is going. Use the cues below to ask questions about your partner's destination. Take notes and ask for any additional information you may need. When you're ready to guess, write the picture's letter in the blank.

| f | g | h | i | j |

rodeado de montañas	playa	clima	ciudad grande o pueblo pequeño	colinas	¿?

El destino de mi compañero/a: _____

3. Show your partner the picture you chose. Did you guess correctly? _____

Look over all the pictures with your partner. Where would each of you really like to travel, and why?

_____

_____

_____

COMMUNICATIVE ACTIVITIES

1. **Situation** You and your partner are discussing the plans you both have made for the near and distant future.

Task Ask your partner when he or she plans to do each thing listed below.

MODELO   A — ¿Cuándo vas al cine?
                 B — Voy al cine cuando llegue mi primo.

ir al cine
ir de vacaciones
casarte
comprar un estéreo
viajar a Europa

2. When your partner asks you when you're going to do each of the things in column A, answer by rewording the information in column B.

MODELO   B — ¿Cuándo vas a encontrar un empleo?
                 A — Voy a encontrar un empleo cuando termine las clases.

A	B
encontrar un empleo	Mi graduación es en junio.
salir de viaje	Todavía tengo dos semanas más de clases.
limpiar tu cuarto	No estoy en casa ahora.
organizar tus apuntes	Tenemos un examen mañana.
visitar a tus parientes en Colorado	Hoy es lunes; voy el lunes próximo.

3. Compare your list with your partner. Who's planning to do more within the next two weeks?

_____

Communicative Activity 12-3B

1. **Situation** You and your partner are discussing the plans you both have made for the near and distant future.

   Task When your partner asks you when you're going to do each of the things in column A, answer by rewording the information in column B.

   MODELO   A — ¿Cuándo vas al cine?
                  B — Voy al cine cuando llegue mi primo.

A	B
ir al cine	Estoy esperando a mi primo.
ir de vacaciones	Todavía tengo clases.
casarte	Busco un empleo.
comprar un estéreo	Me falta dinero.
viajar a Europa	Voy a Europa el 30 o el 31 de julio.

2. Now, ask your partner when he or she plans to do the things listed below.

   MODELO   B — ¿Cuándo vas a encontrar un empleo?
                  A — Voy a encontrar un empleo cuando termine las clases.

   > encontrar un empleo
   > salir de viaje
   > limpiar el cuarto
   > organizar mis apuntes
   > visitar a mi familia en Colorado

3. Compare your list with your partner. Who's planning to do more within the next two weeks?

   _____

Realia and Suggestions
For Using Realia

Contesta estas preguntas y estarás en camino a conocer a la chica o al chico de tus sueños.

Nombres: _____

Apellidos: _____

Fecha de nacimiento: _____

Lugar de nacimiento: _____

Aspecto físico: _____

Pasatiempos: _____

Deportes: _____

Color favorito: _____

Mis pasiones son _____

Soy una persona bastante _____

Si me cumpliera 3 deseos un mago, pediría:

(1) _____

(2) _____

(3) _____

Mis principales atractivos son _____

Lo que más me fascina del mundo hoy en día es _____

Algo que me choca del mundo hoy en día es _____

Mi lugar favorito para visitar es _____

Mi pareja ideal sería _____

_____

¡Felicidades! Estás a punto de convertir tus sueños en realidad...
Conocer a tu pareja ideal te queda a unos pocos pasos.

Realia 1-2

EL VALOR CALORICO DE LAS ACTIVIDADES

ACTIVIDAD	CALORIAS	
	Mujer	Hombre
Caminar (2–3 km/h.)	200	240
Pasear (a 5 km/h.)	240	300
Trabajos caseros (limpiar el piso, barrer, etc.)	300	360
Correr	800	1.000
Escribir a máquina	200	220
Remar	800	1.000
Nadar	600	800
Tenis	440	560
Esquiar	600	700
Leer	40	50
Manejar	120	150
Andar en bicicleta (rápidamente)	460	640
Andar en bicicleta (lentamente)	240	280
Trotar	500	600
Planchar	160	180

Bajar de peso con una dieta solamente, deja los músculos fláccidos. En cambio, si estudias esta tabla recibirás una gran ayuda, porque sabrás cómo ejercitarte para rebajar rápidamente y endurecerte. En ella se indica la cantidad de calorías que consume el cuerpo en una hora de actividad.

Adapted from "El valor calórico de las actividades" from *Tú internacional*, año 11, no. 6, 1990. Copyright © 1990 by **Editorial Televisa**. Reprinted by permission of publisher.

REALIA

Bienvenidos a la programación de

22 de diciembre del 2000

Televista

Canal 11   **El Canal de Las Estrellas**

Tarde

2:00 El Programa de Cristina
con Cristina Saralegui

3:00 A Divertirse con las
Tirillas Cómicas

4:30 El Mundo Submarino de
Jacques Cousteau

6:00 Televista Informa
Edición de la Tarde
con los comentaristas
Donato Mujica y
Rebeca Cubas

Noche

7:00 Telenovela
María de Jorge Isaacs

8:00 Documental Histórico:
Siente Orgullo de
Nuestra Herencia Taína,
Azteca, Inca y Romana

9:00 Variedades Musicales
con Marcia y Rafael Ríos

10:00 Frente a la Política de
Nuestro País con el
Licenciado Calixto Frías

Canal 6   **El Canal Educativo**

Mañana

8:30 Salud y Nutrición
con la doctora Miriam
Cancel

9:00 Las Aventuras de Don
Quijote en Caricaturas

10:00 **La Ilíada y la Odisea**
Comentada por el Pro-
fesor Geraldo Price

11:00 Fútbol Norteamericano
partido repetido de la
semana pasada

12:00 Fútbol Español
Barcelona vs. Celtas

Tarde

1:30 La Vida con Buen Humor
Programa de Entreteni-
miento Cómico

2:00 Maratón de Películas
Vida de Casada
y Vida de Soltera
con Virginia Salado
Nuestra Finca
con Pablo Truco y
Charo Arroyo

4:00 Programa Especial
El Museo del Barrio en
Nueva York

6:00 Noticias Locales e Inter-
nacionales
con Ivonne Mercado y
Tadeo Villalobos

Noche

7:00 Teleteatro: *La Carreta*
de René Marqués

8:00 Navegando la Red
con Elena Richardson

10:00 Temas de Nuestra Juventud
Diálogo entre padres,
educadores, sicólogos y
jóvenes representantes de la
Escuela Modelo José Martí

**Programación sujeta a cambios
de última hora.**

Realia 1-1: Computer dating application

1. **Reading:** Have students look over the form and guess its purpose. Why do they think the form asks the questions it asks? What other questions can students think of that would be appropriate for such a form?

2. **Writing:** Have students fill out the form. Remind them that in many Spanish-speaking countries the date is written in the order *day–month–year*.

3. **Speaking/Pair Work:** Have pairs of students interview each other. The interviewer fills out the form with the other student's responses. Students should switch roles so that each student can practice both asking and answering questions.

4. **Listening:** Dictate the form to the students rather than giving each of them a photocopy. When they have completed the dictation, pass out photocopies of the form for them to check their work.

5. **Culture:** Point out that in Spanish-speaking countries, a boy who wants to go out with a girl usually must meet her family first. During the first date the family will assign a **chaperón** or **chaperona** *(chaperone)* to the young couple. Any member of the girl's family may chaperone the couple— siblings, grandmothers, mothers . . . After the parents get to know the boy well, the couple is normally allowed to go on a date alone. Have students think about why **nombres** and **apellidos** are plural. Remind students that many Spanish speakers have a first name (**nombre de pila**), a middle name, an **apellido paterno**, and an **apellido materno**.

Realia 1-2: Chart of calories burned

1. **Reading:** Ask students to place each **actividad** into one or more of the following categories: **deportes, quehacer, trabajo, pasatiempo**

2. **Writing:** Have students write sentences saying how often they do each **actividad. (siempre, a veces, nunca)** Have them calculate how many calories they burn on a typical Saturday.

3. **Pairwork/Speaking:** Have students tell each other about three sports or pastimes they practice and three they like to watch on TV.

4. **Listening:** Read aloud some of the sentences the students wrote in Activity 2, and have the class guess who wrote them.

5. **Culture:** Explain that young Spanish speakers practice sports to be healthy. Also point out that their everyday diet contains an abundance of fresh fruit and vegetables. Point out that people in the Spanish-speaking world are not necessarily as preoccupied with weight loss as are Americans.

Holt Spanish 2 ¡Ven conmigo!, Chapter 1

Realia 1-3: TV schedule

1. **Reading:** Have students skim the **Televista** schedule trying to guess what type of program each one is: **documental, deporte, telenovela...**

2. **Listening:** Have students cover the **Televista** schedule as you read aloud some of the programs. **(Don Quijote en muñequitos, Variedades musicales, Nuestra finca, Temas de Nuestra Juventud...)**. Ask them to use an expression of like or dislike **(me choca, me encanta, me fascina)** for each program. To check for comprehension, occasionally ask a student to justify his or her answer. **El mundo submarino de Jacques Cousteau: Me gusta porque me fascinan los documentales.**

3. **Writing/Speaking:** Divide the class into groups of three. Have students work together to write an ideal TV schedule and express why they chose each program, using expressions of like and dislike.

4. **Culture:** You might tell students that Mexican soap operas **(telenovelas)** are very popular and are mostly shown during peak viewing time. Furthermore, Mexico produces the largest number of **telenovelas** and exports them throughout the world. These **telenovelas** are known for their high quality. Point out that, unlike soap operas produced in the U.S., **telenovela** series come to a conclusion. They last anywhere from two to four months.

Realia 2-1

AL MAL TIEMPO...BUENA CARA

Es muy normal que en algún momento de nuestras vidas nos sintamos deprimidos. Quizás puedas reconocer las formas en que se manifiesta el monstruo: te sientes muy cansado, te falta ánimo, cambias constantemente de buen humor a mal humor, te sientes triste con mucha frecuencia, etc. Hay ocasiones en que resulta bien difícil deshacerte de este monstruo. Para poder controlarlo necesitas seguir los siguientes pasos:

▶ **Debes hacer ejercicios.**
Los ejercicios te ayudan a relajarte y estimulan la circulación de oxígeno al cerebro. Así puedes pensar más claramente.

▶ **Tienes que llevar una dieta nutritiva.**
Si comes alimentos nutritivos tu cuerpo se conserva sano. Te sentirás menos cansado y tendrás ganas de enfrentar tus problemas.

▶ **Haz trabajo de voluntario para una organización de ayuda a la comunidad.**
Si compartes tu tiempo y te mantienes ocupado te vas a sentir más contento y más útil. Recuerda, tú tienes mucho que dar y no tienes tiempo para quedarte deprimido.

▶ **Elimina la tristeza y el sentirte víctima.**
Sal y relájate con tu mejor amigo o amiga. Cuéntale tus problemas pero, ¡cuidado! No abuses de su confianza. Demuéstrale que tú puedes superarte y que escuchas sus buenos consejos.

▶ **Rodéate de buenas amistades.**
La idea es distraerte y pasar el rato en compañía de los buenos amigos. Esta técnica es muy popular y es la que tiene mayor éxito para despejar la mente. No te quedes solo con tus preocupaciones. Vístete bien y ve a divertirte con tus amigos.

Lista de cotejo

Tener una lista de todo lo necesario para el viaje es la mejor garantía para contar en su momento con un equipaje completo. Siempre conviene hacerlo con bastante anticipación para no olvidarse de nada: las sorpresas es mejor reservarlas para la aventura. En este listado, cada cosa debe registrarse con una marca de cotejo.

DOCUMENTACIÓN

Debe llevarse fotocopia de todos los documentos.

PERSONAL

❑ Pasaporte
❑ Certificado de vacunación
❑ Visados

SEGURIDAD

❑ Tarjeta de crédito
❑ Cheques de viajero
❑ Listado de embajadas españolas
❑ Datos personales y domicilio permanente
❑ Cartera cinturón

CALZADO

❑ Botas: deportivas o de marcha
❑ Zapatos de lona
❑ Sandalias
❑ Calcetines térmicos, de lana o de algodón

PARA EL FRÍO

❑ Abrigo
❑ Guantes
❑ Bufanda
❑ Cazadora o chaqueta

SALUD

❑ Reconocimiento médico
❑ Seguro de viaje
❑ Vacunas
❑ Crema protectora para el sol
❑ Gafas de repuesto

EQUIPAJE

❑ Mochilas
❑ Riñonera
❑ Maletas
❑ Maletín

ROPA

❑ Camisas de manga larga de algodón
❑ Camisas de manga corta de algodón
❑ Pantalones cortos y largos
❑ Bañador
❑ Cinturón
❑ Sombrero
❑ Gafas de sol
❑ Jersey
❑ Chaquetón

Adaptation of text from "Check List" from catalog, *Viajes y Aventuras*, no. 6, Spring/Summer 1994. Reprinted by permission of **Coronel Tapioca 2, S.A.**

R E A L I A

Realia 2-3

Gente joven de Puerto Rico y España

Sonia y Gabriel nos presentan su país de origen y nos hablan de su patria chica.

Sonia Nieves, Barranquitas

¡Hola! Me llamo Sonia Nieves. Tengo 17 años. Soy puertorriqueña. Puerto Rico es una isla preciosa en el Mar Caribe. En general el clima en Puerto Rico es agradable todo el año. Yo nací en San Juan pero vivo en Barranquitas. El pueblo se llama así porque está en las montañas y tiene muchas barrancas pequeñitas. Hace mucho fresco en el pueblo, pues estamos a 2,788 pies de altura sobre el nivel del mar. Como las distancias en Puerto Rico son cortas, a mi familia y a mí nos fascina ir a la playa todos los fines de semana. A mí también me gusta salir a divertirme con mis amistades. En San Juan puedes hacer de todo: nadar, caminar, bailar, ir al teatro o simplemente conversar con los amigos en una de sus plazas. Debo confesar que yo soy bien fiestera y me encanta divertirme sanamente con mis amistades y también con mis padres.

Gabriel Zengotita, Pamplona

¡Qué tal! Soy Gabriel y tengo 18 años. Me encanta mi país y la ciudad donde vivo—Pamplona, la capital de la región de Navarra. Mi ciudad es muy moderna pero a la misma vez conserva edificios antiguos de la Edad Media. En la zona histórica está la catedral gótica que fue reconstruida en 1397. Otro edificio que vale la pena ver es el mausoleo del Rey Carlos III. Aquí hay muchas cosas que uno puede hacer, como nadar, pescar, ir a los bosques y caminar por la ruta de la peregrinación de Santiago. En el invierno hace bastante frío y tenemos mucha nieve. A mí me encanta esquiar en la nieve. Modestia aparte soy un experto en este deporte. Claro que si vives al lado de los Pirineos tienes que ser un experto.

REALIA

Realia 2-1: Magazine article about how to fight depression

1. **Reading:** Have the students skim the article looking for phrases that indicate positive feelings and attitudes: **buen humor** *(good mood)*, **pensar más claramente** *(to think more clearly)*, **distraerte** *(to have a good time)*, **pasar el rato en compañía de buenos amigos** *(to spend time in the company of good friends)*, **despejar la mente** *(to clear one's mind)*, **ve a divertirte** *(go have fun)*, **te vas a sentir más contento y más útil** *(you are going to feel happier and more useful)*.
2. **Listening/Writing:** Read the expressions of positive feelings and attitudes aloud and ask the students to write an English equivalent of each one. If they're not sure, tell students to guess, then discuss their reasoning and help them find the best English definition.
3. **Writing/Speaking:** Divide the class into groups of three and ask them to write in Spanish five essential techniques to overcome the "blues."
4. **Culture:** You might explain that Hispanic people express different degrees of sadness using **estoy** and expressions such as **así así** *(so-so)*, **más o menos** *(all right)*, **medio triste** *(kind of sad)*, **muy triste** *(very sad)*, **tristísimo/a** *(extremely sad)*.

Realia 2-2: Checklist from catalogue

1. **Listening/Speaking:** Read a series of items on the list. Students respond by saying what sort of store or office they would need to visit to buy some of the items you mention.
2. **Reading:** Have students read over the checklist and guess the meaning of any unfamiliar words. Ask them what sort of trip they would need this list for. *(an adventure trip in a foreign country)* What is meant by the advice, "**las sorpresas es mejor reservarlas para la aventura**"? *(Plan well for your trip to avoid any unpleasant surprises.)*
3. **Writing: a.** Tell students to imagine that they are preparing for a trip but don't have time to do everything they need to do to get ready. Have them write a note to a friend or family member asking him or her to help with some of the preparations. They should list specific preparations their friend should make.
b. Each student selects a travel destination. Students then use the checklist as a model to create their own list of things they need to pack and places they need to go to prepare for the trip.
4. **Speaking/Pair Work:** Divide the class into pairs. Have each pair choose one or two categories from the list. One student reads the items in the chosen category and asks the other student if he or she has taken care of it yet. The second student responds by saying whether or not he or she has already done it.
5. **Culture:** Explain to students that in some Spanish-speaking countries there are arrangements between the government and the private sector to provide students with substantial discounts for traveling within their own country. These discounts apply mainly to buses and trains. Usually, students stay at hostels (**hostales**) which are very inexpensive. If the student is younger than 18 years of age, he or she needs to present a letter from his or her parents giving permission for the trip. Generally, minors travel in groups with one or more of their teachers.

Realia 2-3: An invitation to visit Puerto Rico and Spain

1. **Reading:** Have students create a list with the following categories: **tiempo** *(weather)*, **paisaje** *(landscape)*, **atracciones** *(attractions)*, **información histórica** *(historical information)*. Ask them to list the various features of each place in the appropriate category. Then ask them to compare Barranquitas and Pamplona, based on their findings.

2. **Writing:** Ask students to write a brief description of their city or town. Have them use words and phrases from the **Vocabulario** on page 61, and ask them to include information from the four categories in Activity 1 above.

3. **Listening:** Read short descriptions of Barranquitas, Pamplona, and your hometown, and have students say which city you are describing.

4. **Pairwork/Speaking:** Have students work with a partner to describe the ideal city where they would like to live as an adult.

5. **Culture:** Skiing is a popular sport in South America. People go to ski resorts at Valle Nevado and Portillo in Chile, or Las Leñas in Argentina. In Central America camping in the rain forest of Costa Rica is a favorite recreational activity. In Honduras, boating, scuba diving, and snorkeling off the island of Roatana are popular. In Spain, one of the most colorful events is the running of the bulls in Pamplona. The most popular sports in all Spanish-speaking countries are soccer, baseball, and basketball.

Un Día En La Vida De Un Campeón

Martín López Zubero

Nombre: Martín López Zubero
Deporte: la natación
Edad: 27 años
Cumpleaños: 23 de abril
Nacionalidad: español y estadounidense
Lugar de nacimiento y domicilio actual:
Jacksonville, Florida

Martín López Zubero nació en Estados Unidos, de padres españoles. Por eso tiene doble nacionalidad; es español y estadounidense. Tiene, hasta la fecha, 17 récords mundiales y en 200 espalda no hay nadie mejor en el mundo.

Se levanta temprano

Martín se levanta temprano, a las cinco y media de la mañana. A las seis ya está en la piscina. Pasa dos horas nadando antes de desayunar.

Es la rutina de todos los días y durante todo el año.

¿Qué come?

Los atletas tienen que dormir y comer bien. Martín se acuesta temprano para poder levantarse otra vez a las cinco y media. En cuanto a la dieta, los atletas deben comer mucha fruta, legumbres, hidratos de carbono en forma de patatas, pasta, arroz, pan y cereales. Beben agua, mucha agua, y jugos de frutas. Bueno, ya sabes cómo es la vida de un gran deportista. ¿Crees que puedes llegar a ser un campeón?

Realia 3-2

El Mundo Imparcial

CLASIFICADOS

304 DOMÉSTICOS

Ama de llaves–Para cocinar y hacer la limpieza general de la casa. Dormir en colocación. Área del Condado. De lunes a sábado y los domingos libres. Si le interesa favor de llamar al tel. 002-0003 Familia Sr. Rodrigo Ricardo

Estudiante–¿Quieres trabajar? ¿Necesitas dinero para tus estudios? Mi agencia **Ayuda Doméstica** te da la oportunidad de ganar dinero extra los fines de semana. Necesitamos muchachos y muchachas para cuidar el jardín, regar las plantas, barrer las aceras y el garaje, y para hacer los quehaceres domésticos: pasar la aspiradora, trapear los pisos, lavar los platos, sacudir el polvo, tender las camas, etc. Si te interesa favor de llamar a Lynda al tel. 111-4444

Personas para la limpieza–Restaurante área de San Juan está buscando personas que quieran trabajar haciendo labores domésticas. Tenemos trabajo para personas que quieran barrer y trapear los pisos (conserjes), para lavar los platos (lavaplatos), para ayudar en la cocina cocinando y para quitar y poner las mesas en el salón comedor. No necesita hacer cita previa. Si le interesa favor de pasar de lunes a viernes por la Calle Sol núm. 2097B, Restaurante El Castillo. Pregunte por doña Janet o don Felipe

REALIA

ENTREVISTA

Miguel García es un jugador de tenis. Él tiene 16 años de edad y se considera buen estudiante aunque reconoce que las matemáticas es la materia más difícil para él.

Desde los 6 años de edad está con una raqueta de tenis y es tanto el gusto que le saca que desde esa edad ya ha estado compitiendo. Todos los martes, jueves y sábados se entrena.

Para que nuestros lectores lo conozcan un poco lo invitamos a que nos cuente de su vida.

Aparte del tenis, ¿qué otras cosas te gusta hacer?
Me encanta tocar la guitarra y el piano. También me gusta leer y mirar la televisión.

¿Qué haces cuando no te entrenas?
Juego al fútbol y al voleibol con mis compañeros del colegio.

¿Qué haces los fines de semana?
En general, practico el piano y la guitarra. A veces mis amigos y yo nos reunimos y vamos al cine o al centro comercial.

¿Eres una persona disciplinada?
¡Claro que sí!

¿Tienes hermanos?
Sí, tengo una hermana y un hermano mayores que yo.

¿Quiénes son tus mejores amigos?
Pablo, Chela y Bárbara, mis compañeros de la escuela.

¿Sigues entrenándote después de un campeonato?
Sí, generalmente me entreno dos días a la semana.

¿Qué fue lo que más te gustó de tus compañeros de las competencias?
La unión con los compañeros, por hacer todo juntos y entrenarnos juntos.

¿Tienes algún mensaje para los niños?
Si les gusta un deporte, deben practicarlo, ser constantes y disciplinados.

Así es Miguel, un niño serio y tenaz para quien el tenis es una cuestión de disciplina, gusto y rapidez. Todos debemos practicar un deporte para ser sanos y fuertes.

REALIA

Realia 3-1: Interview

1. **Reading:** Have students go over the article and answer the following questions: **¿Por qué es famoso Martín López Zubero? (Es campeón de natación) ¿Dónde vive Martín? (Jacksonville, Florida) ¿Cuántas nacionalidades tiene? (Dos) ¿Cuáles son? (Es español y estadounidense).**

2. **Speaking:** Divide the class into pairs and have students tell each other Martín López Zubero's daily routine, from memory, sticking as close as possible to the routine stated in the article.

3. **Listening/Writing:** On the board, or on a transparency, write the following headings: **Actividades, Comida, Identidad.** Divide the class into teams of 4 or 5, and have each team choose a scribe. The scribe writes the categories on a piece of paper. As you read the article, the team prompts the scribe to write the important words or phrases under the appropriate heading. The team with the most correct items wins.

4. **Culture:** Many Hispanic celebrities in the United States were born in other countries, or are the children of immigrants. For example, Gloria Estefan was born in Cuba but came to the United States as a young girl. **Salsa** singer Mark Anthony and actress Jennifer López have Puerto Rican parents.

Realia 3-2: Newspaper classified ads

1. **Reading:** As a prereading activity, divide the class into groups of three. Have students list the household chores they think they would like to do in order to earn extra money. Each group should discuss the activities they like, those they dislike, and how often they could do each one. Then ask students to read the classified ads.

2. **Writing:** Have small groups of students cooperatively write a classified ad similar to one of those in the realia.

3. **Speaking:** Divide the class into pairs. Each partner will take turns telling the other which chores he or she should do, and the other will respond with a complaint.

4. **Listening:** Read the classifieds aloud and ask the students to identify in which room or rooms of the house each activity can be carried out.

5. **Culture:** In Spanish-speaking countries, the classifieds are still one of the main means of finding jobs or hiring employees. Those looking for employment search in two main areas: the government and the private sector. Most announcements include information about applying —for example, whether to fill out an application, write a letter showing interest in the position, or submit a résumé.

Realia 3-3: Interview with tennis player Miguel García

1. **Reading:** Have students read the **Entrevista.** Who is being interviewed? **(Miguel García)** ¿Cuántos años tiene? **(16 años)** ¿Cuánto hace que juega al tenis? **(10 años)**

2. **Writing:** Have students write an **Entrevista** feature on themselves. They should answer the same or similar questions as were asked of Miguel, substituting a sport or hobby that interests them.

3. **Speaking:** Divide the class into pairs. One student is the interviewer, the other is being interviewed. Interviewers should ask questions about the interviewee's interests, hobbies, and daily routine. The interviewer should be sure to ask how long the interviewee has participated in any sports or hobbies the interviewee mentions.

4. **Listening:** Read the **Entrevista** feature aloud to the class. Then ask the questions that were asked of Miguel in third-person form (*i.e., Aparte del tenis ¿qué otras cosas le gusta hacer?*) and have the class report what Miguel's answers are (i.e., **Le gusta leer y mirar la televisión**). You may want to paraphrase some of the interview questions to better incorporate functions from the chapter, for example, "**¿Cuánto tiempo hace que Miguel se dedica al tenis? ¿Qué le gusta hacer en sus ratos libres?**"

5. **Culture:** In Spanish-speaking countries it is not uncommon for young people to have several very different hobbies. Many young people are devoted to a sport such as soccer, basketball, or dance. At the same time, they may play a musical instrument or play chess. Their free time is balanced between physical and intellectual activities.

REALIA

Realia 4-1

Academia Pedro Albizu Campos
Calle Betances # 322
Culebras, Puerto Rico

Nombre del Alumno: López Cancel, Zuleyka
Primer Semestre: agosto-diciembre de 1998

Asignaturas	Asistencia	Conducta	Tareas	Calificaciones
Español	96%	Excelente	100%	A = 98.5
Inglés	100%	Buena	80%	B = 86
Arte (Pintura)	100%	Excelente	97%	A = 98
Geometría	80%	Buena	70%	C = 75
Navegando la Red (Internet)	98%	Buena	75%	B = 80.5
Música	80%	Buena	70%	C = 75

Comentarios:

Firma del Docente

Rosario Arroyo

Firma del Director

Casildo García Santiago

Firma del Padre o Encargado

Sonia Noemí López

REALIA

*N*ombre:

Enrique Iglesias Preysler. Nació el 8 de mayo de 1975, en Madrid. Tiene 22 años y es tauro. Mide 1,90 m y pesa 80 kg. Reside en Miami desde los 7 años, si bien reconoce que se siente "español por los cuatro costados". Dejó los estudios de Empresariales, que cursaba en la universidad de Miami, en segundo curso.

*F*amilia:

Es hijo del superfamoso cantante Julio Iglesias y la no menos conocida Isabel Preysler, la "reina de las revistas del corazón." Tiene dos hermanos famosos: Chabeli, modelo y presentadora de televisión, y Julio José, actor y muy pronto también cantante. Y tres hermanos pequeños: Tamara, Ana y Miguel Alejandro.

*P*ersonalidad:

Detrás de esa imagen de chico intransigente y rebelde se esconde un hombre sensible y solitario, "muy cariñoso, entrañable y tímido," como él mismo reconoce. Le gusta "disfrutar de las cosas simples de la vida, y de los momentos con mi familia y con mis amigos".

R E A L I A

Realia 4-3

Excursiones
Huatulco Bonito

Reservaciones para las excursiones

Llene la hoja de inscripción con su nombre, hotel donde se hospeda, y su número de habitación. Marque con una equis (X) las excursiones a las que piensa ir, la fecha cuando piensa asistir y la forma de pago. Regrese la hoja de inscripción al representante de Excursiones Huatulco Bonito en nuestra oficina en el pasillo del hotel. Si necesita más información fuera de nuestro horario regular, por favor llámenos a nuestra oficina central: 1–22–50

Nombre:_____ Hotel:_____ Hab:_____

Forma de pago. Favor de indicar con una (X):
Dólares__ Cheques de viajero__ Tarjeta de crédito__ Pesos__

Días de excursión Fecha de asistencia	Excursión	Hora	Precio por persona
diario _____	¡A conocer la ciudad! almuerzo y cena incluidos	11:00–7:00	180.00
diario _____	¡Vamos de compras! almuerzo y merienda incluidos	9:00–4:00	1800.00
diario _____	La cultura mexicana: Oaxaca almuerzo y merienda incluidos	10:00–5:00	180.00
vier./sab./ dom. _____	Las siete bahías en Huatulco almuerzo y merienda incluidos	9:00–3:00	1800.00
diario _____	¡Vamos a bucear, a pescar y a pasear en bote! almuerzo incluido	10:00–4:00	1900.00
vier./sab./ dom. _____	¡Montemos a caballo! Vista escénica de la ciudad	9:00–1:30 2:00–4:30	700.00

R E A L I A

Realia 4-1: Report card

1. **Reading/Writing:** Have students skim the grade report and write in their note-books any words they cannot identify: **conducta** (*class behavior*), **docente** (*teacher*), **director** (*principal*), **encargado** (*tutor*). Ask them to guess the meaning of each new word.

2. **Listening:** Read the **asignaturas** aloud and ask students to number each one in the order you read them: **arte, pintura, español, navegando la Red, geometría, inglés, música.**

3. **Speaking:** Divide the class into pairs and ask them to give Zuleyka three suggestions on how to get better grades in some of her classes.

4. **Culture:** The use of computers and the World Wide Web is becoming more and more important in Spanish-speaking countries. Some useful terms: **el servidor** *(server)*, **el site** *(the site)*, **atrás/regrese** *(back)*, **adelante/siguiente** *(foward)*, **virtual** *(virtual)*, **cibernético** *(cyber)*, **salas de conversación/charla** *(chat rooms)*, **pulse/oprima/haga click** *(click)*. Some of the most interesting places to visit are the **cibercafés**. To visit a **cibercafé**, students can just surf the Net and be in a café in Bolivia or some other Spanish-speaking country!

Realia 4-2: An interview with Enrique Iglesias

1. **Reading:** Divide students into four groups. Have students read the text and look up unfamiliar words in the dictionary. Ask students the following reading comprehension questions: **¿Cuántos años tiene Enrique? ¿De dónde es? ¿Dónde vive o reside? ¿Cómo se llama su papá? ¿Cuántos hermanos tiene? ¿Cómo es Enrique?**

2. **Speaking/Writing:** Ask each group to discuss and to list what they think are the three most important items from each section of the reading. Write on the board the headings: **Nombre, Personalidad,** and **Familia.** Then have each group name a representative to write under the appropriate heading the three items selected by their group.

3. **Listening:** Read aloud the items written on the board in number 2. Ask students to cover the realia or turn it face down as you read the reading aloud, one section at a time. As you finish each section, ask students to indicate the appropriate heading: **Nombre, Personalidad,** or **Familia.**

4. **Culture:** Many young idols in the Spanish-speaking music world are the children of famous parents. Like Enrique Iglesias (the son of the famous Spanish singer Julio Iglesias), another top-of-the-chart singer—Cristian Castro—the son of Mexican actress, producer, and talk-show host Verónica Castro. Alejandro Fernández is the son of Vicente Fernández, a famous Mexican **ranchero** singer. All these young artists have recognized the guidance, support, and love their parents have given them. Their parents have expressed how proud they are that their children chose the same profession. Both generations have indicated the important role family has played in their success.

R
E
A
L
I
A

Realia 4-3: Tourism brochure

1. **Reading:** Have students read the brochure and name as many water sports as they can: **bucear** (*to dive*), **pescar** (*to fish*), **pasear en bote** (to *go boating*).

2. **Writing/Speaking:** Divide the class into groups of three. Ask them to write their four favorite activities and explain why these interest them. Have them discuss this with their partners.

3. **Listening:** Read aloud an itinerary and have students underline the day trip they would like to take: **¡A conocer la ciudad!** (*Lets see the city!*), **¡Vamos de compras!** (*Let's go shopping!*), **¡Montemos a caballo!** (*Lets go horseback riding!*)

4. **Culture:** Oaxaca has been rich in cultural heritage since pre-Colombian times. Indians make up one-third of the state's population. Benito Juárez, the most famous **oaxaqueño,** was the first Indian to become president of Mexico (in 1858). His famous quote **El respeto al derecho ajeno es la paz** (*Respect for the rights of others is peace*), is widely known throughout Mexico.

Nombre _____ Clase _____ Fecha _____

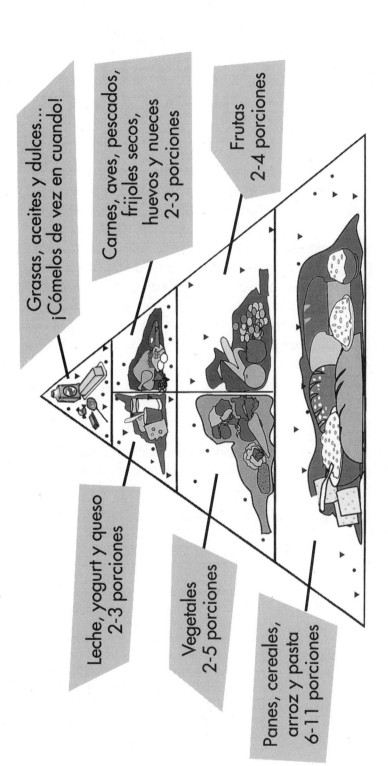

Grasas, aceites y dulces...
¡Cómelos de vez en cuando!

Carnes, aves, pescados,
frijoles secos,
huevos y nueces
2-3 porciones

Frutas
2-4 porciones

Leche, yogurt y queso
2-3 porciones

Vegetales
2-5 porciones

Panes, cereales,
arroz y pasta
6-11 porciones

CLAVE
• Grasas (naturales y adicionales)
▶ Azúcares (adicionales)

Estos símbolos indican grasas y azúcares presentes en los alimentos

Fuente: Departamento de Agricultura y Departamento de Salud y Servicios Humanos de los Estados Unidos

R E A L I A

Realia 5-2

¿CÓMO PUEDE EVITARSE EL CÁNCER EN LA PIEL? SÓLO CON SENTIDO COMÚN

La piel actúa como un filtro que protege su organismo de la radiación, las sustancias químicas dañinas y las infecciones. Anualmente se reportan más de 400,000 casos de cáncer de la piel, el órgano más grande de su cuerpo. Cuando se descubre a tiempo el cáncer de la piel es curable pero lo mejor de todo es que este cáncer se puede evitar. La doctora Tatiana Joel les da consejos a los jóvenes para mantener una piel sana y libre de cáncer.

La exposición en exceso a los rayos del sol trae como consecuencia el cáncer de la piel. No tenga miedo, pues no es necesario eliminar las actividades al aire libre para disminuir la probabilidad de desarrollar cáncer de la piel. Al trabajar o divertirse use su sentido común y protéjase adecuadamente. Las quemaduras solares frecuentes son particularmente peligrosas. Hoy en día el estar bronceado sale muy caro, pues puede costarle la vida.

Cúbrase. Con un sombrero de ala ancha y un pañuelo para el cuello; use camisa o blusa de manga larga y pantalones que el sol no pueda penetrar. Las sombrillas y los filtros solares también pueden ayudarlo pero es mejor combinar todos los métodos para estar bien protegido.

No tome píldoras que aceleren el brocearse ni use lámparas de luz ultravioleta. Tome solamente el sol a las horas donde los rayos del sol son más débiles y evite tomar el sol entre las 11:00 a.m. y las 2:00 p.m., ya que los rayos del sol son más fuertes durante estas horas.

Examine su piel. Asegúrese que conoce su tipo de piel: muy clara, aceituna, rosada, morena u oscura. Haga un mapa de su piel y tome nota mental de los nuevos lunares, manchas y verrugas. Si observa cambios de color, forma, tamaño o encuentra una llaguita que no sana, vaya a ver a su médico inmediatamente. Recuerde que Ud. puede combatir este cáncer si se protege del sol y está al tanto de los cambios en su piel. No se desanime, la palidez está de moda.

Holt Spanish 2 ¡Ven conmigo!, Chapter 5   Activities for Communication **97**

Realia 5-1: Food pyramid

1. **Reading/Writing:** Have students study the food pyramid. From each food group, ask students to write the three foods they eat most often.

2. **Speaking:** Divide the class into pairs and have them advise each other about things they should eat to be healthy.

3. **Listening:** Read the following words and ask students to point to the corresponding food group: **dulces** *(candies)*, **aceite de oliva** *(olive oil)*, **pollo** *(chicken)*, **frijoles** *(beans)*, **arroz** *(rice)*, **pasta** (pasta), **frutas** *(fruits)*, **leche** *(milk)*, **vegetales** *(vegetables)*, **huevos** *(eggs)*.

4. **Culture:** The Aztecs had a varied, balanced, and nutritious diet. It included fruits and vegetables such as aguacate *(avocado)*, **camote** *(sweet potato)*, **jícama** *(a turnip-like root)*, green and red **tomate** *(tomato)*, **maíz** *(maize)*, **huautli** *(amaranth)*, **cebollas silvestres** *(wild onions)*, several kinds of **calabacitas** *(squash)*, **chiles** *(chilies)*, several varieties of **tunas** *(prickly pears)*, **guayabas** *(guava)*, and **maguey** *(a kind of agave)*. They also consumed bird eggs and various meats, such as turkey, pig, duck, venison, and rabbit. They also utilized fish and algae from the lake in their cuisine. One of their favorite and nutritious drinks was what they called chocolatl, which in Spanish became **chocolate**.

Realia 5-2: Article on how to avoid skin cancer

1. **Reading:** Have students read the article on how to avoid skin cancer and underline sentences with negative commands: **No tenga miedo** *(Don't be afraid)*, **No tome píldoras que aceleren el broncearse ni use lámparas de luz ultravioleta** *(Don't take pills to enhance tanning and don't use ultraviolet lamps)*; **No se desanime** *(Don't get discouraged)*.

2. **Speaking/Writing:** Divide the class in groups of three. Have them discuss, and write down, five things people should do to avoid skin cancer.

3. **Listening:** Read aloud the following statements and ask students to indicate whether or not the statement is good advice for preventing skin cancer: **Use un sombrero de ala ancha** (Sí); **Sufra de quemaduras de sol** (No); **Use un pañuelo para el cuello** (Sí); **Utilice la sombrilla y el filtro solar** (Sí); **Tome píldoras que aceleren el broncearse** (No); **Tome el sol a las 2:00 de la tarde** (No); **Use su sentido común** (Sí).

4. **Culture:** Have students do research in the local library or use the Internet to find out about skin cancer rates in Spanish-speaking countries. Also have them think about how proximity to the equador might affect those statistics.

Realia 5-3: Cartoon

1. **Reading**: Have students read the cartoon and look for the explanation given in the cartoon: **Lo lamento chicos, me voy al pueblo a ver si llegó correspondencia.** *(I'm sorry, guys. I'm going to town to see if there's any mail)*.

2. **Listening/Writing**: Divide students into three groups. Ask each group to revise the dialogue in the cartoon by writing new chores and new explanations for why they can't do them. **Bueno chicos, tienen que preparar ensalada para 200 personas esta noche**. After peer-editing, read each bubble aloud and have students guess which frame it corresponds to.

3. **Speaking**: Divide the class into small groups, and have each group come up with a creative list of reasons why they can't do every chore mentioned in the cartoon: peeling potatoes, washing dishes, removing pits from olives, and helping the campers. Then have groups compare their explanations and vote on the most original, the most believable, the funniest, etc.

4. **Culture**: In Latin America, in addition to the **usted** and **tú** forms, there is another second person singular: **vos**. The **voseo**, the use of **vos**, is common in southern Mexico, throughout Central America, and in Argentina. Usage varies. In Argentina, **vos** is used to address friends and strangers alike. In Central America, **vos** implies a deep sense of familiarity and closeness. In Guatemala and in Southern Mexico, a child would use **vos** with his siblings, close friends, and parents, but would use **tú** with uncles and aunts and **usted** with teachers and older people in general. To conjugate a verb in the **vos** form; drop the "r" from the infinitive and add an accent and an "s". For example: **querer querés**; **decir decís**.

R E A L I A

Realia 6-1

Lugares de interés para visitar:
1. Plaza de Armas
2. Iglesia de San Francisco
3. Palacio de la Torre Tagle
4. Plaza Bolívar
5. Plaza San Martín
6. Paseo de Aguas
7. Plaza de Ancho
8. Museo de Arte
9. Museo de Larco Herrera
10. Hotel El Olivar
11. Hotel los Delfines

Map from brochure, *Lima Guide* by H. Stern Peru, S.A. Reprinted by permission of **H. Stern Peru, S.A.**

Holt Spanish 2 ¡Ven conmigo!, Chapter 6

Viaje a San Antonio

Impreso por: **Calixto Frías**   30 de marzo de 1999 11:00 AM
Título: **Viaje a San Antonio**   Página 1 de 1

 El 30 de marzo de 1999 10:00 AM

DE :   Enery García
TÍTULO : Viaje a San Antonio
PARA :   Calixto Frías

Querido Calixto:

¡Hola! Te escribo este correo electrónico para contarte sobre mi viaje a San Antonio con mis padres. Primero que nada, debo decirte que tomamos el avión en Dallas a las 8:00 de la mañana. Fue un viaje de apenas 45 minutos. Nos hospedamos en un hotel cerca del Paseo del Río. Fuimos a desayunar a un restaurante mexicano. Yo pedí migas con salsa verde y mis padres, tacos de fajitas. Empezamos nuestro recorrido paseando en las lanchas que van por los canales del Paseo. Luego fuimos a La Villita, que es como un centro comercial mexicano. Papá compró un sombrero mexicano y Mami se compró un traje muy bonito. Yo te compré un regalo. Cali, ¡San Antonio es precioso! Tienes que venir a visitar esta ciudad. Después fuimos a la Torre de las Américas para cenar y tomar fotos desde el observatorio. ¡La vista es impresionante! Durante nuestras vacaciones en San Antonio fuimos al Alamodome a ver dos partidos de baloncesto. Papá y yo nos divertimos mucho. Por último te cuento que los chicos son guapos pero no tan guapos como tú. ¡Me haces mucha falta! Mañana salimos para Puerto Rico. El avión llegará como a las 4:30; espero verte en el aeropuerto.

Un beso,

Enery

R E A L I A

Realia 6-3

Restaurante La Carreta

Servimos desayuno de las 7:30 a las 11:00 y hasta las 12:30 los domingos.

PARA EL DESAYUNO

Pan tostado con mermelada	3.50
Cereales con plátano	3.75
Huevos rancheros	6.75
Migas	6.75
Migas especiales con hongos	8.00
Huevos con jamón o tocino	6.50
Omelet de jamón y queso	6.50

ANTOJITOS MEXICANOS

Quesadillas	6.50
Tostadas de pollo	8.50
Chilaquiles	5.50
Queso flameado	4.75
Nachos	6.50

SOPAS

Sopa del día	3.30, 5.00
Consomé de pollo	3.30, 4.20
Sopa de tortilla	4.20, 7.75
Sopa de ajo	3.00, 4.00

ENSALADAS

Ensalada de lechuga y tomate	3.00
Ensalada de aguacate	4.00

SANDWICHES

Jamón	8.25
Jamón y queso	9.00
Queso	6.25
Hamburguesa	9.00
con queso	9.75
Club sándwich	10.50

*Servimos las entradas con ensalada
o arroz y frijoles.*

CARNE DE RES

Filete mignon	26.00
Filete a la pimienta	24.00
Puntas de filete	22.00
Hígado a la italiana	12.00

CARNE DE CERDO

Lechón asado	16.50
Chuletas de cerdo	14.00
Costillas de cerdo al B.B.Q.	22.00

PESCADO

Pescado del día a la parrilla	*precio del mercado*
Huachinango a la veracruzana	20.25
Huachinango al ajillo	20.25

POLLO

Pechuga de pollo a la milanesa	16.00
Pollo frito	12.00
Arroz con pollo	12.00
Pechuga de pollo a la plancha	14.00

POSTRES

Plátanos con crema	5.00
Flan de la casa	3.50
Arroz con leche	2.75
Pastel de chocolate	5.25

BEBIDAS

Refrescos	1.60
Jugo de naranja natural	3.00, 6.00
Jugo de tomate, piña o toronja	2.50
Vaso de leche	1.50
Café americano	1.25
Café espresso	3.25
Capuccino	4.00
Chocolate caliente	3.00
Té caliente o helado	1.50
Limonada	2.00

A LA CARTA

Tamales	
de cerdo	1.25
de verduras	1.00
Papas fritas	2.00
Arroz mejicano	2.00
Arroz blanco	1.00
Frijoles refritos	2.00
Frijoles charros	2.00
Aguacate	2.50

*Aceptamos tarjetas de crédito. Un 15%
de servicio será agregado a grupos de más
de 7 personas.*

Holt Spanish 2 ¡Ven conmigo!, Chapter 6

Realia 6-1: Mapa de Lima, Perú

1. **Listening:** Ask the class, "**¿Dónde tengo que bajarme del autobús para ir al Museo de Arte?**" Students should respond by saying the name of a nearby street or intersection "**Para ir al Museo de Arte debes bajarte en (el Paseo Colón).**"

2. **Reading:** Have students look over the city map. What clues can they find to help them figure out what part of the world this city is in? (Plaza San Martín, Hotel Bolívar, and some street names indicate that this city is probably in South America) What clues can they use to tell what city this is? (Catedral de Lima)

3. **Writing:** Tell students they have won a week's vacation in Lima, Peru. Have them study the map to decide which places they would like to visit and which hotel they will be staying in. Then have them write a note to the hotel concierge asking how they should travel to reach the places they want to visit.

4. **Speaking:** Divide the class into pairs or small groups. One member of each group is the concierge at the Hotel Savoy, the other students are guests at the hotel. Students ask the concierge to recommend local attractions and explain how to get to them. Students switch roles.

5. **Culture:** Lima, the capital of Peru, is one of the most beautiful colonial cities in South America. It was established by Francisco Pizarro on January 18, 1535. It is now a very prosperous city that blends the splendor of the past with the innovative architecture of a modern city. People from Lima are called **limeños.** Some of the most beautiful colonial buildings are **el Palacio de Gobierno, la Casa de la Moneda,** and **la Catedral de Lima.** The **Catedral** was finished in 1625 and had to be rebuilt after the devastating earthquake of 1746. To admire the art of Peru, one can visit the **Museo de Arte Colonial,** the **Museo de Antropología y Arqueología,** or the **Museo de Pintura.** One of the most distinctive characteristics of Peruvian architecture, dating from the colonial times, is the **balcones limeños.** These balconies are made of dark wood and carefully carved to give the impression of a delicate piece of lace.

Realia 6-2: Electronic mail

1. **Reading:** Have students read the e-mail and list the preterite verbs they can identify. Also, have them make a list of the places in San Antonio visited by Enery and her family.

2. **Listening:** Read the letter aloud and ask the students true-false questions to test their comprehension.

3. **Writing:** Have students write a brief e-mail about what they did during their vacations, modeling their work on the realia.

4. **Pair work/Writing:** In pairs, have students imagine that they work for their local government tourist office, and write an e-mail to Enery trying to convince her to come to their hometown or city.

5. **Culture:** In Puerto Rico, **turismo local** or **doméstico** is the term used to refer to travel within one's own country. Most domestic tourist travelers are families. Many travel agencies cater to this segment of the population, paying special attention to activities appropriate for all ages. Many of the vacationing families include at least one grandparent, as well as young children. The peak season for **turismo local** varies from country to country. In Puerto Rico, the heaviest season for **turismo nacional** is during Easter week and in the summer. In Hispanic countries, Christmas is generally not considered a season for tourism, although many people travel at this time of year. At Christmas people usually travel to be with family and are less likely to use tourist services or visit tourist spots.

Realia 6-3: Restaurante La Carreta

1. **Listening:** Ask the class "**¿Cuánto cuesta (una comida de pollo frito con arroz y frijoles, una orden pequeña de sopa de tortilla y una ensalada de aguacate)?**"

2. **Reading:** Have students read over the menu. Which foods are familiar? Which are unfamiliar? Can they guess what some of the unfamiliar foods are?

3. **Writing:** Have students write a script for a skit entitled "**Lo que me pasó una tarde en el Restaurante La Carreta.**"

4. **Speaking:** Divide the class into pairs or small groups to enact a typical restaurant scene. One student in each group is the server, the others are customers. Students switch roles.

5. **Culture:** Mexican cuisine is rich and varied. For Mexicans, cooking is a link to their indigenous American cultural heritage. Every region has a distinctive cuisine.
   * the North: **tortillas de harina** (*flour tortillas*), **cabrito** (*goat*)
   * the Central Highlands and Mexico City: **chilaquiles** (*hot shredded tortillas baked with heavy cream*), crema de **cuitlacoche** (*a fungus that grows on corn*), **sopa de flor de calabaza** (*squash blossom soup*)
   * Puebla and Michoacán: **mixiotes** (*meat wrapped in maguey leaves and cooked barbecue style in an earthen oven*), **pozole** (*a soup made with pork and hominy corn*)
   * the Gulf Coast: **huachinango a la veracruzana** (red snapper cooked with tomato sauce, capers, olives, and other spices)
   * Oaxaca and the Southeast: **mole negro** (*a chocolate sauce made with chili peppers, burned tortillas and other spices*)
   * Yucatán: **cochinita pibil** (*a spiced pork dish*)

   Ask students to locate on a map of Mexico the different culinary regions. You may want to distribute copies of the map of Mexico from Map Transparency, page 5.

INFANCIAS ALGO IMAGINARIAS
Guión: Meiji.
Dibujos: O'Kif

HOY:
ALBERT EINSTEIN

El 14 de marzo de 1879 nació en Ulm, Alemania, Albert Einstein.

El chico mostró gran afición por las ciencias.

¡Da!

En los juegos de la infancia no dejaba de evidenciar su vocación científica.

Estoy trasladando la pelota a quince kilómetros por hora y unos cinco centímetros del piso.

¡Pasála de una vez Albert, no seas morfón!

También se daba el tiempo para cometer alguna que otra travesura en la casa.

¡Si la agarro a tu tía Frida que te regaló esos crayones, la mato!

¡Siempre escribiendo pavadas vos!

$E = mc^2$

A los diez años ingresó en el instituto Luitfold de Munich.

¿QUERÉS SER PREMIO NÓBEL? ESTUDIÁ EN NUESTRA ESCUELA

Cálculos.

● Albert Einstein recibió el premio Nóbel de física en 1921 y entre numerosos descubrimientos fue el impulsor de la teoría de la relatividad.

● ¿Qué elementos hay en la historieta que no corresponden a la época?

REALIA

Realia 7-2

25 de septiembre

Querida nieta:

¿Cómo estás? Espero que estés bien junto a tus compañeras de cuarto en la Universidad de Texas. Tus padres me leyeron tu carta electrónica y ya ves, aquí estoy, usando el viejo método. Ahora estás conectada a Internet y prefieres usar el correo electrónico antes de escribirme una carta. En realidad la computadora de tus padres me vuelve loca. Yo prefiero seguir usando la máquina de tu abuelo. Pienso que los carteros necesitan comer regularmente. Debo admitir que no soy inmune a los cambios y oigo mis artistas favoritos en discos compactos.

Cuando yo tenía tu edad sólo escuchábamos música en las emisoras de radio. La mayor parte del tiempo la pasábamos charlando, visitando amistades o familia. Claro que de vez en cuando había un baile. Tú sabes que me fascina bailar. Tu abuelo y yo nos conocimos en una fiesta de Carnaval en la Casa España en San Juan.

¡Aquéllos eran otros tiempos! La gente se conformaba con pocas cosas. Yo nunca soñé con pedirle un carro a papá para mi cumpleaños. En esa época a las mujeres no se les permitía manejar un coche. Camila, tú recibiste el primer coche cuando tenías 17 años. Ahora tienes un carro deportivo rojo, descapotable y con aire acondicionado. Tantos adelantos me hacen sentir vieja. Yo he visto tantos cambios en mi vida, buenos y malos. Ojalá que el amor y el respeto hacia las personas no cambien nunca. Te quiero mucho y estoy muy orgullosa de ti. Espero verte pronto. Un beso y un abrazo.

Te quiere,

Abuelita María

Noticias de Éxito

Sintonízate a la música buena que lleva un mensaje positivo.

Feliz como una lombriz...vuelve Ricky Martin

El 24 de febrero Ricky Martin lanzó su nuevo disco a nivel mundial. Este lleva por título "Vuelve". El disco contiene trece canciones; entre ellas están el tema del próximo mundial de fútbol, que se celebra esta vez en Francia. En su disco Ricky incluye baladas románticas como "Sin ti" y "Casi un bolero" entre otras. Ricky Martin ha pegado mucho últimamente con su gran éxito "María". En su nueva aventura discográfica la canción "La bomba" va a ser el nuevo éxito bailable del talentoso puertorriqueño.

Christopher Reeve es tan bueno como un ángel y tiene amigos tan nobles como un perro

El concierto "Celebración de la esperanza" se celebró en la Ciudad de Los Ángeles para brindar apoyo al actor Christopher Reeve. El famoso actor que interpretó por muchos años al Hombre de Acero (Superman) tiene una fuerza de voluntad férrea. La parálisis no puede parar sus deseos de mejorar su salud o estado físico. Varios de sus amigos aportaron su talento y su buena voluntad para hacer del concierto un verdadero éxito, entre ellos: Robin Williams, Paul McCartney, Stevie Wonder y Willie Nelson. La nobleza de estos artistas y la belleza de sus corazones son dignas de elogio.

REALIA

Realia 7-1: Einstein cartoon

1. **Reading/Pair work:** In pairs, have students read the story of Einstein and say three or four things he used to do when he was young. Encourage them to use **Primer paso** vocabulary from page 219 of the textbook.

2. **Listening:** Tell students about things you used to do when you were a child, using vocabulary from page 219 of the textbook. Have students write each imperfect verb form they hear.

3. **Speaking/Writing:** Divide the class in groups of three. Have each person in the group find out what the others used to do when they were ten years old. You might want to display a transparency with the question **¿Qué hacías cuando tenías diez años?** Students should take notes and be prepared to report their findings to the rest of the class.

4. **Culture:** You might tell students about people in Latin America and Spain who have won the Nobel Prize. Most recipients have won medals for their literary work or for their efforts for peace. Some of the winners for literature are: **Octavio Paz** (Mexico), **Gabriel García Márquez** (Colombia), **Gabriela Mistral** (Chile), **Pablo Neruda** (Chile), and **Camilo José Cela** (Spain). **Rigoberta Menchú** of Guatemala won the Nobel Peace Prize in 1992 for her peaceful campaign for indigenous peoples' rights. Another Nobel Peace Prize winner is **Óscar Arias Sánchez** of Costa Rica. He won the prize for his efforts to end wars in Central America.

Realia 7-2: Grandmother's letter

1. **Reading/Speaking:** Have students read the letter. Tell them to think of at least two things that have changed in the last five years. They should use **Segundo paso** vocabulary found on page 219 of the textbook, and they should be prepared to report their findings to the class.

2. **Writing:** Have each student write a short paragraph about what life used to be like when he or she was six years old. To help students focus on chapter-related themes, tell them to mention utilities, houses, food, clothes, etc.

3. **Speaking/ Pair work:** In pairs, have one student play the role of a nature lover and have the other pretend to be a "city slicker." The nature lover will remember how things were in the countryside while the city slicker will remember how things were in the city. Encourage students to use **Segundo paso** vocabulary. Ask students to share their memories with the rest of the class.

4. **Culture:** In the old days in Spanish-speaking countries, young girls in the first stages of courtship used the language of the fan to send secret messages. In Puerto Rico, doña Felisa Rincón de Gautier (1897–1994) —the first woman to be elected mayor of San Juan— was a master of the **lenguaje del abanico** *(language of the fan)*. She believed that the art of this language should not be lost, so she educated the public about its meaning. She said that a suitor could tell immediately the fate of the relationship by the way his beloved moved the fan. For example, if the woman touched her cheek with the fan, she was telling her admirer that she found him attractive. On the other hand, if she fanned herself fast and ignored the suitor, that meant she was not interested.

Realia 7-3: Ricky Martin and Christopher Reeve article

1. **Reading/Speaking:** Using phrases from **Tercer paso** vocabulary (see page 219 of the textbook), have students describe the two performers in Realia 7-3.

2. **Writing:** Have students write a short essay about a Latin American entertainer, describing the artist and his or her work.

3. **Reading:** Have students read the articles in Realia 7-3 and answer the following questions: **¿Por qué es famoso Ricky Martin? ¿Cuáles son algunas de sus canciones más famosas? ¿Cuál fue el rol más importante de Christopher Reeve? ¿Quiénes son algunos de sus famosos amigos? ¿Por qué son sus amigos "tan nobles como un perro"?**

4. **Culture:** Many Latin American and Spanish artists have been able to "cross over" to the United States market and develop successful careers in the arts. These artists not only strive for excellence in such fields as music and acting, but they also have become role models for Latino youth in the United States. Some of them are: Puerto Rican singer **Ricky Martin**, tejano star **Selena**, actresses **Salma Hayek** and **Jennifer Lopez**, and actor **Antonio Banderas**. You may want to ask your students if they can think of other artists and singers. Some examples are Andy García, Gloria Estefan, Tito Puente, Luis Miguel, and Enrique Iglesias.

Realia 8-1

Fechas para celebrar

2 noviembre

Día de los muertos en México

En México celebran este día de una forma muy especial. En muchas casas se construyen altares con ofrendas para los familiares muertos. Sobre una mesa ponen la foto del familiar y muchos adornos. Los adornos más comunes son cerámica y flores. Las ofrendas son sobre todo pan y comida. También hacen calaveras y otras figuritas con pasta de azúcar. Cantan y bailan canciones alegres y divertidas porque para ellos éste es un día de fiesta.

Altar mexicano con ofrendas

25 diciembre

Día de Navidad

La Navidad es una fiesta cristiana muy importante tanto en España como en Latinoamérica. Esta celebración conserva muchas tradiciones. Una de ellas es pedir el aguinaldo. Consiste en ir de casa en casa cantando villancicos y deseando Felices Pascuas a los amigos. En agradecimiento éstos les dan un aguinaldo, que es un regalo de dulces o monedas.

28 diciembre

Día de los Santos Inocentes

Un día como hoy, hace unos 2000 años, un rey llamado Herodes mandó matar a muchos niños inocentes. De ahí viene el nombre de este día. Pero el tiempo cambió las lágrimas de pena por lágrimas de alegría. Y ahora, en los países hispanos, éste es el día de las bromas.

13 diciembre

Martes y trece: Mala Suerte

En los países hispanos se dice: "Trece y martes, ni te cases ni te embarques". ¿Sabéis por qué? Porque, según la tradición, éste es el día de la mala suerte.

21 diciembre

Verano en el Cono Sur

Este día se celebra el comienzo del verano en el Cono Sur, formado por Argentina, Chile y Uruguay. En estos países el sol brilla todo el año pero durante esta época se sobrepasan los 40 grados. ¡Qué calor!

31 diciembre

Noche Vieja

¿Noche triste o alegre? Eso depende de si tú eres una persona optimista o pesimista. Nosotros somos muy optimistas y pensamos que éste va a ser un año estupendo.
Una costumbre española es comer doce uvas al tiempo que dan las campanadas de fin de año. Si lo consigues, dicen que tienes un año feliz.

Palabras

la broma - *joke*   **la campanada** - *ring of a bell*   **disfrutar** - *to enjoy*   **en vivo** - *live*
la lágrima - *tear*   **la ofrenda** - *gift*   **los seguidores** - *followers*   **ser capaz de** - *to be able*
sobrepasar - *to exceed*

"Fechas para celebrar" page 3 from *Ahora*, vol. 1, no. 2, November/December 1994. Copyright © 1994 by **Scholastic, Inc.** Reprinted by permission of the publisher.

¡*No dejes para mañana lo que puedes hacer hoy!*

Lista de mandados:

1. poner gasolina al carro
2. pasar por el banco
3. comprar estampillas
4. mandar una carta
5. comprar medicinas

** TELEBANCO 4B **

REF.   0072.0404.60

FECHA   HORA   OPERACION DEPO/AUT
15/08/99   14:26   728

TARJETA NUM. . 590049 1032 01513103/0

IMPORTE
RETIRADO   ******60.00€

GRACIAS POR SU VISITA

REALIA

Realia 8-3

El euro

es la moneda oficial de la Comunidad Europea

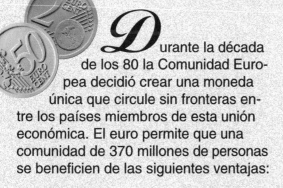

Durante la década de los 80 la Comunidad Europea decidió crear una moneda única que circule sin fronteras entre los países miembros de esta unión económica. El euro permite que una comunidad de 370 millones de personas se beneficien de las siguientes ventajas:

- una moneda en común para todo el mundo
- la simplificación de las transacciones financieras
- estabilización de los precios
- intereses más bajos
- la posibilidad de una moneda que compita con el yen y el dólar

El euro tiene como propósito fortalecer a Europa económicamente y simplificar las relaciones comerciales entre los países de la Comunidad Europea. Comenzando en el 1999, los bancos, las compañías y las bolsas de valores han estado comerciando en euro.

Los billetes del euro son siete. Cada billete tiene un color y un formato que corresponde a su valor: 5 – gris, 10 – rojo, 20 – azul, 50 – naranja, 100 – verde, 200 – marrón y 500 – morado. El euro tiene un símbolo en común en un lado y en el otro un símbolo único para representar cada país. Desde el 2002 en adelante se usa el euro como moneda oficial en España.

Realia 8-1: Fechas para celebrar

1. **Reading:** Have students read about the different holidays. Ask students: Why are these days special? What kinds of things are placed on the altars on November 2nd? What do people do for good luck on December 31st?

2. **Writing:** Have students write a journal entry as if they had attended a celebration for one of the holidays they read about. They should include how they felt, and whether there is a similar celebration in the U.S.

3. **Speaking:** Divide the class into groups. One member of each group (Student A) will describe a holiday or how he or she celebrated a holiday, without mentioning it by name. The other students will try to guess which holiday is being described.

4. **Listening:** Ask student volunteers to read what they wrote in their journal entry (exercise 2 above). Then have another student volunteer recount what the students said.

5. **Culture:** In the United States, New Year's Eve is a time to go out with friends and have a party. In Latin America, **La Noche Vieja** is considered a family affair. Every country has different traditions, but one constant is that families meet to have a traditional meal, talk about the events of the last year, and welcome the beginning of a new year together. In Mexico, everyone wears red as a symbol of good luck in the new year. In Puerto Rico, some families have **asopao de pollo**, a traditional chicken soup, just after midnight. Ask your students to share their family's traditions for the last day of the year, including special foods, meaningful symbols, and styles of celebration.

Realia 8-2: Don't put off until tomorrow what you can do today

1. **Reading/Writing:** Have students read the list of things to do in Realia 8-2. Ask them to write a list of five things they have to do using **Primer paso** vocabulary from page 215 of the textbook.

2. **Speaking/Pair work:** Using the lists of chores students created in the previous activity, have them explain to a partner why they were unable to do at least two of those tasks. Encourage the class to use phrases like **Esperaba...**, **Quería pero no pude porque...**, and **Tenía que...**

3. **Listening:** Give students a list of seven tasks that you need to do this weekend. Have them listen to your list and write down four tasks they also need to do.

4. **Culture:** You might want to point out to your students that in cities across the United States life seems to move very fast in comparison to life in Latin America. For example, in Mexico, families have lunch together every day. After lunch, everyone takes a **siesta**. A large part of the city comes to a stop because stores, offices, and banks do not open until everyone comes back from the afternoon **siesta**. This tradition allows people to rest, relax, and spend quality time with their families.

R
E
A
L
I
A

Using Realia 8-3

Realia 8-3: Euro news

1. **Reading:** Ask students to read the realia and answer the following questions: ¿Cuáles son las ventajas de usar el euro? ¿Cuáles son los colores que se usan en el euro? Si tienes un billete verde y uno rojo, ¿cuántos euros tienes? ¿Qué moneda usa España?

2. **Listening:** Have students say how many euros you have based on the color of the bills. For example, you could say: **Tengo dos euros amarillos y uno marrón. ¿Cuántos euros tengo?** Students should write down the total number of euros in Spanish.

3. **Writing:** You might want to have students write a short paragraph suggesting a new design for the dollar bill. What design would they use and why? Remind them that the amount should be easily recognizable, the design should be safe against counterfeiters, and the artwork should illustrate the culture and history of their country.

4. **Pair Group/Speaking:** Divide the class in groups of four. Have each group draw a new design for the dollar bill and present it to the class. Students can vote for the most interesting design.

5. **Culture:** You can point out to students that the graphic art on the euro bills reflects "eras and styles in Europe." The architectural styles shown focus on seven periods of European cultural history: classical, romantic, gothic, Renaissance, baroque, rococo, and the twentieth century. Architectural elements such as gates, windows, and bridges symbolize the openness and cooperation of the member states. The euro bills were designed by Robert Kalina, an employee of the Austrian National Bank, whose designs were chosen from 43 proposed designs.

R E A L I A

MUSEO DE ANTIOQUIA

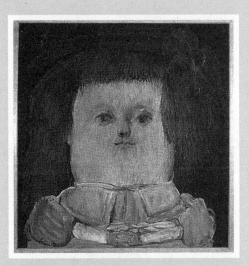

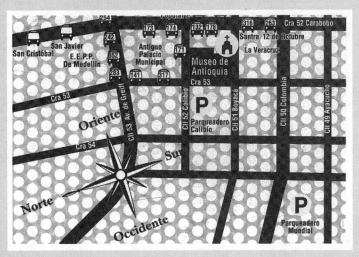

HORARIOS: Sede principal, martes a viernes 9:30 a.m. a 5:30 p.m. Sábados 9:00 a.m. a 2:00 p.m. **Cerrado:** domingos y días festivos. **Sede Alterna,** lunes a viernes 8:00 a.m. a 12:00 a.m. y 2:00 p.m. a 6:00 p.m. Sábados 8:00 a.m. a 2:00 p.m. Cerrado: domingos y días festivos. **Entrada:** El ingreso al **Museo de Antioquia** tiene un costo muy bajo, que varía cada año.

MUSEO DE ANTIOQUIA Cra 52A No. 51A29 • SEDE ALTERNA Cra. 45 (El Palo) No. 52 49
Medellín Colombia
RUTA INTERNET: HTTP://WWW.EAFIT.EDU.CO/MDEA/MDEA/HTML
RUTA AUTOPISTA ELECTRONICA: HTTP://WWW.EDUCAME.GOV.CO

Map from brochure, *Museo de Antioquia.* Reprinted by permission of **Museo de Antioquia.**

R E A L I A

Realia 9-2

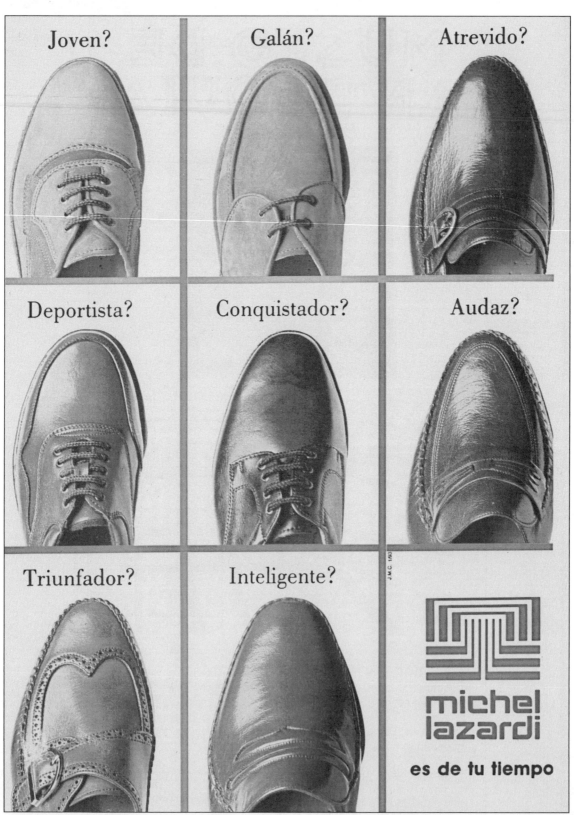

Joven? Galán? Atrevido?

Deportista? Conquistador? Audaz?

Triunfador? Inteligente?

michel lazardi

es de tu tiempo

Advertisement for "Michel Lazardi" from *Eres, año* VII, no. 161, March 10, 1995. Reprinted by permission of **J.M. Comunicaciones.**

Querida Kathy:

¿Cómo estás? ¿Cómo están tus padres y tu hermanito Donald?
Nosotros estamos muy bien. Papá empezó a trabajar y casi no
tiene tiempo para nada. Mamá y yo vamos de compras casi
todos los días. Siempre vamos con Octavia; ella es la encargada
del servicio doméstico en nuestra nueva casa. Es una señora
muy inteligente y muy buena gente. Octavia es una experta
regateando y siempre trata de buscar rebajas. Hoy compramos
piñas, calabazas y plátanos con un 25% de rebaja. Mamá está
aprendiendo a regatear también. Ayer mamá compró unos
floreros y algunos artículos de cerámica para abuelita en el
mercado al aire libre. Aprende este pequeño dialógo para cuando
nos visites en enero. Iremos a buscar gangas por toda la Ciudad
de México.

Mamá—¿En cuánto me deja este florero?
Vendedor—En 10,000 pesos señora.
Mamá—Está muy caro. ¿Me puede hacer una rebaja?
Vendedor—Se lo doy por 9,550 pesos.
Mamá—No, le doy 8,075.
Vendedor—Es muy poco. Se lo regalo por 9,500 y no bajo más.
Mamá—Gracias, me lo llevo.

¿Qué te parece mi español? Puedo decir que soy bilingüe, ¿no?
Aquí en México todo el mundo me trata bien y aunque a veces
digo disparates, la gente no se ríe de mí. Todos tratan de
ayudarme y enseñarme español. Tienes que venir a visitarnos
en enero. Tengo muchos amigos nuevos y quiero que los
conozcas. Escríbeme pronto.

Chao,
Nancy

REALIA

Realia 9-1: Museum brochure

1. **Reading:** Ask students to look for the following information: the museum's telephone number, address, Internet address, and times that the museum is open during the week.
2. **Listening/Pair work:** In groups of two, have students give directions to the museum. Partner 1 will ask where the museum is, and Partner 2 will give directions on how to get there from the **Parqueadero Mundial.** Once Partner 2 has finished, Partner 1 will repeat the directions to make sure he or she can get there.
3. **Writing:** Using **Primer paso** vocabulary, have students write directions from their Spanish classroom to different locations in the school. For example, you can suggest that they give directions from the Spanish classroom to the library, or from the classroom to the gym. You may want to give them time to write the directions and then pair them up so they can peer-edit their work.
4. **Community:** Have students call a local museum and ask for the address, telephone number, Internet address, price of admission and the museum's operating hours.
5. **Culture:** In the United States, when you ask someone for directions they are very likely to give the names of streets and main roads. You can also buy a map and find exactly where you want to go. In Latin America, directions are often given using landmarks. For example, you may be referred to nearby buildings, plazas, supermarkets, or fountains.

Realia 9-2: Shoe store ad

1. **Reading:** Have students read the advertisement and answer the following questions. What aspect of the product or store does the advertisement emphasize? How does it do this? Do you think this advertisement is effective in achieving its intended goals? Why or why not? Does it make you want to shop in this store?
2. **Writing:** Have students price the products shown in the realia and create their own advertisements.
3. **Speaking:** Divide the class into small groups. One member of each group is a salesperson at the store, the others are customers shopping for shoes.
   a. The salesperson should offer to help the customers find what they are looking for.
   b. The customers respond appropriately.
   c. The salesperson then shows them shoes in the advertisement that he or she thinks they might like.
   d. They express their opinion about the shoes and give their shoe size based on the conversion chart on page 265 of the textbook.
   e. Students comment on how the shoes look and fit.
4. **Listening:** Describe some of the shoes featured in the advertisement to the class. As students listen they should try to determine which shoes are being described.
5. **Culture:** In Latin America people take good care of their shoes. In any plaza one can find a person who shines shoes for a moderate price. People also take their worn shoes to a **zapatería** where a professional **zapatero** can replace the soles or repair a hole. Leather bags and suitcases are also repaired rather than discarded.

Realia 9-3: Letter from Mexico

1. **Reading:** Have students read Nancy's letter and answer the following questions: ¿Qué compraron en el mercado? ¿Quién regateó? ¿Qué dijo? ¿Cuánto dinero ahorró la mamá de Nancy? ¿Quién va a visitar a Nancy en enero?

2. **Pair Work/Speaking:** Have pairs of students create a short dialogue. Partner 1 is buying some food in the local open-air market and wants to buy only bargains. Partner 2 is the owner of the food stand, and does not like to have clients ask for discounts. Remind both partners to remain courteous and keep each other's good will, as they will see each other in the market again.

3. **Listening:** You may want to talk about your experiences in an open-air market. Tell students what you bought and how much you paid for it. Have them list the items and write out the price.

4. **Culture:** Point out to students that open-air markets are very common in Latin America. They can buy just about anything at very good prices. Bargaining is part of market culture and vendors usually expect it. Prices are not fixed, so there is always room to make a deal. The prices in regular stores are fixed, and students should not expect to bargain there. Ask students to compare garage sales in the U.S. with open air markets. What is the same? (You can buy just about anything, bargaining is expected.) What is different? (Used items versus new, ongoing market versus one-time only sales.)

Realia 10-1

2. YOLOUCA O EL PÁJARO QUE NACIÓ DEL ARCO IRIS

Cuando el cielo concluye su lamento, y la franja de los siete colores adorna el verde profundo de los cerros, los hombres recuerdan su pasado.

Recuerdan el día en que el silencio de la tierra convocó los vendavales y las tormentas. Árboles, animales y hombres fueron arrastrados a los mares profundos; lagos y ríos desbordados cubrieron llanuras y valles; las bestias corrieron, huyendo del desastre; las reses rugían sumergiéndose en la angustia; peces y aves navegaron unos en el agua y otros en el aire, buscando refugio; antílopes, zorros, y monos treparon a los árboles.

El más terrible desorden reinó en la tierra.

Pasaron los días y la fuerza de las aguas creció. El mundo se había convertido en un mar inmenso. De la tierra no quedaban más que dos o tres colinas nevadas, a punto de ser cubiertas.

Los sobrevivientes: algunas mujeres con sus niños y sus hombres, y varias parejas de animales, pedían misericordia y piedad con sus vidas a los dioses.

A los cuarenta días el clamor se tornó en una forma que surgió de la oscuridad. Era una sombra iluminada, que desde la lejanía se acercaba. Su visión era claridad y consuelo. Los últimos habitantes de la tierra lloraron, esperanzados. La presencia divina se hacía más clara y cercana. En el tercer día se convirtió en un anciano luminoso y sereno. Era un mensajero del cielo que habló así: — De los seres y las cosas, ustedes son los últimos de la tierra. Tienen por esto la misión de sobrevivir. Deberán embarcarse en una canoa construida con el esfuerzo de todos y esperar que Yolouca aparezca en la inmensidad. Sólo hasta ese día cesarán las tormentas y la tierra se recuperará de la furia de la naturaleza.

Emprendieron la tarea de construir la rudimentaria nave. De los árboles caídos y de las fuertes hojas de los cañaverales, los artesanos tejieron una segura y ágil barcaza, que pronto fue la habitación de animales y hombres.

Mucho tiempo después que todo esto sucedió, un silencio detuvo las tormentas... Las nubes fueron apartadas suavemente y el sol iluminó las aguas. El cielo se tiñó de un verde indescriptible y en el firmamento un tejido de arco iris de colores cubrió la tarde.

De los colores se desprendió un pájaro multicolor. Era Yolouca, el mensajero de los dioses. Su vuelo era un espectáculo de gracia, esperanza y vida. Su canto se unió al de los náufragos y los guió hasta la única orilla del inmenso lago.

Allí, cada ser buscó refugio. Al cabo de los años el tiempo mejoró y la tierra fue más fértil. Los animales se desplazaron a todos los lugares de la tierra, conformando familias diferentes y variadas. Los hombres, agradecidos, fundaron pueblos. La vida brotó de nuevo en el planeta.

Adapted from "Yolouca, o el pájaro que nació del arco iris" from *Mitos y Leyendas Latinoamericanas*. Copyright © 1990 by **Educar Cultural Recreativa S.A.** Reprinted by permission of publisher.

REALIA

Realia 10-2

INFANCIAS ALGO IMAGINARIAS

Guión: Meiji
Dibujos: O'Kif

HOY: NAPOLEÓN BONAPARTE

Napoleón Bonaparte nació el 15 de agosto de 1769 en Ajaccio, en la isla de Córcega, perteneciente a Francia.

O sus delirios de dominio, poder y fama

También podemos jugar al monopoly y al estanciero.

¡Noooo!

La manía de andar con una mano atrás y otra adelante le empezó desde muy pequeño.

Cuentan los historiadores que se mostraba siempre muy querendón.

¡Josefina, je t'aime!

¡Ay, Napoleón, vos siempre tan conquistador!

El colmo de su vanidad la mostró esa mañana de domingo

¡Nene! ¿Qué estás haciendo con las hojas de laurel para el tuco?

Su ansia de poder lo acompañó durante toda su vida y podemos afirmar que siempre la tuvo re-clara.

¿Para qué tanto lío? Cuando sea grande me hago nombrar emperador y listo.

El presidente de un país lejano busca su re-reelección.

● Napoleón Bonaparte expandió los dominios de Francia desde Moscú hasta Lisboa. En 1804 fue coronado emperador en la catedral de Notre Dame de París.

● ¿Qué elementos encontrás en la historieta que no pertenecen a la época?

R E A L I A

Realia 10-3

■ **Genética**

Tranquilo como papá, genial como mamá

Cierta actriz le dijo un día al dramaturgo irlandés Bernard Shaw: "Con su inteligencia y mi belleza, imagine qué hijos podríamos tener! "Ya—replicó el autor, que era muy feo—, pero suponga que heredasen mi belleza y su inteligencia." Y no le faltaba razón. Eric Keverne y Amiz Suranim, de la Universidad de Cambridge, han realizado un estudio en ratones de laboratorio en el que analizaron los genes etiquetados —esto es, siempre reconocibles gracias a una etiqueta bioquímica—de la madre o del padre.

A partir de él se intenta demostrar que la herencia genética materna juega un papel primordial en la formación de la inteligencia de la prole, mientras que en la constitución del carácter prevalece el patrimonio genético del padre.

¿De la madre se hereda la inteligencia y el carácter, del padre?

REALIA

Realia 10-1: Yolouca legend

1. **Reading:** Read the story aloud as a listening comprehension activity. Or, you can place the following questions on the board or on an overhead transparency and have students answer them in short sentences. **¿Cuál era el problema de los habitantes de la tierra? ¿Qué les dijo el mensajero del cielo? ¿Qué construyeron los habitantes de la tierra? ¿Qué hizo Yolouca? ¿Qué pasó finalmente?**

2. **Pair work/Writing:** In pairs, have students create and illustrate a legend. Each legend should have four illustrations, and students should write three sentences for each one. Remind students to use connectors to make their story more interesting. To encourage creativity, you may want to tell students to use **Segundo paso** vocabulary as a source of ideas.

3. **Writing/Listening:** You may want to make two lists on the board. One side can be labeled *Imperfect* and the other *Preterite.* Choose a fairy tale and prepare two sets of questions for each column. Ask the students questions and write their answers under each category, based on the verb form(s) used in the answers. **¿Qué hizo Blanca Nieves con la manzana? Blanca Nieves se la comió. ¿Dónde estaban los enanitos? Ellos estaban trabajando fuera de la casa.** When this exercise is finished, you may want to have students prepare a composition in which they tell the story, using the verbs on the board and connectors.

4. **Culture:** One of the most famous legends in Mexico is the story of the founding of the great city of Tenochtitlán. The legend says that the Aztecs were unhappy with their land, and a god promised to give them land that was great and beautiful. The god also said that after a long journey they would find an eagle sitting on a cactus with a serpent in its mouth. The Aztecs began their journey south until they reached what is today the Valley of Mexico. As they were exploring the area, they saw the divine sign and decided to build the city of Tenochtitlán, which later became Mexico City. Ask students to briefly summarize and provide other examples of legends about the founding of a city. (Romulus and Remus)

Realia 10-2: Napoleon cartoon

1. **Reading/Writing:** Have students read the comic strip story about Napoleon and make a list of the things he used to do when he was a child. You may want to provide students with a list of verbs to use.

2. **Listening/Pair work:** In pairs, have students talk about what the weather was like during their last two vacations. You can write the following questions on the board: **¿Adónde fuiste en tus últimas vacaciones? ¿Qué tiempo hacía?** Students can use the **Primer paso** vocabulary on page 311 of their textbook.

3. **Group work:** Have students work in groups of four. Each group will rewrite the story of Napoleon from the following points of view: **la maestra, Josefina, el amigo,** and **la mamá.** They can choose their characters and tell the story using the **Primer paso** vocabulary on page 311 of the textbook.

R E A L I A

4. **Listening:** Tell students a brief story about your childhood and have them make a list of the preterite and imperfect verbs they hear.

5. **Culture: El Niño** is a weather disturbance characterized by the warming of the surface waters in the tropical Pacific Ocean that affects the normal weather patterns. **El Niño** was first noticed toward the end of the nineteenth century by fishermen off the coast of Peru. Since it takes place around Christmas it was named **El Niño**, which in Spanish refers to the *Christ child*. A weather disturbance of unusually cold currents in the summer is called **La Niña**. When there is a particularly bad year of **El Niño** during the winter, **La Niña** usually appears in the summer. Ask students how ocean currents near South America can have such a profound effect around the planet. (Changing wind circulation and moisture patterns can lead to severe flooding, drought, and other drastic changes that affect agriculture, transportation, and many other aspects of life.)

Realia 10-3: Magazine article about inherited characteristics

1. **Reading:** Have students read the article and answer the following questions about the story. **¿En qué universidad hicieron este estudio? ¿Por qué se llama el artículo "Tranquilo como papá, genial como mamá"? ¿Cómo son tus padres? ¿Cómo eres tú?**

2. **Group work/ Writing:** In groups of four, have students look in Spanish newspapers or on the Internet for interesting news. Have them bring two headlines to class. Each group should prepare a three-line summary of each headline. You may want to prepare a handout with the headlines and have the rest of the class react to the summaries using **Tercer paso** vocabulary on page 311 of the textbook.

3. **Listening:** You may want to bring to class some excerpts of a Spanish newscast and ask students to react to the stories. Encourage them to use the expressions on page 300 of the textbook.

4. **Culture: Tertulias** are discussion groups in which friends or strangers gather to discuss the latest headlines, literature, or politics. In Latin America, a **tertulia** can take place in a cafe, a restaurant, or a plaza. Young people have a genuine interest in politics and social issues, so they tend to be involved in **tertulias** and often debate ideas vigorously. Ask your students if they are interested in news and if they read the newspapers or online news services. You may also want to encourage them to begin their own **tertulias.**

Nombre _____ Clase _____ Fecha _____

JAGUAR (Panthera onca)
Selva Maya de la Península de Yucatán

FLAMENCO
(Phoenicopterus ruber)
Humedales de Yucatán

ÁGUILA ELEGANTE
(Spizaetus ornatus)
Selva Zoque de Veracruz y Chiapas

MEXICANOS EN PELIGRO

Bonitos ¿verdad? Míralos bien, porque estas especies están en peligro de desaparecer por la destrucción de su habitat.
Adopta con PRONATURA a cualquiera de estos mexicanos en peligro; tu donativo es deducible de impuestos.

PAVÓN
(Oreophasis derbianus)
Bosques de niebla en Chiapas

PRONATURA

PRONATURA, A.C.
Apartado postal 19–223 -México-03901 D.F.
http://www.pronatura.org.mx
email:pronatura@compuserve.com

BORREGO CIMARRÓN
(Ovis canadensis)
Península de Baja California

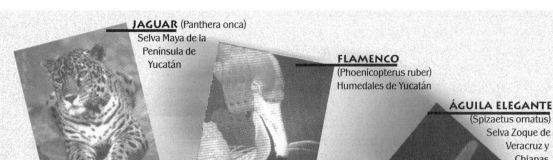
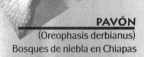

REALIA

Realia 11-2

TÚ Y EL
MEDIO AMBIENTE

La destrucción del medio ambiente preocupa a los habitantes de todas las regiones de la Tierra. ¿Y a ti? ¿Te preocupa? ¿Tratas de conservarlo o no? Contesta honestamente a las siguientes preguntas.

1. **¿Qué es la ecología?**
   a) El estudio de los ecos.
   b) Una rama de la física.
   c) El estudio del medio ambiente.

2. **Estás comiendo unos dulces. ¿Qué haces con la envoltura?**
   a) La echas a la basura.
   b) La metes en tu bolsillo junto con todos los otros trozos de papel que has acumulado.
   c) La tiras al suelo.

3. **Compras algo en unos grandes almacenes. ¿En qué insistes?**
   a) En que te den una bolsa de papel.
   b) En que te den una bolsa de plástico.
   c) En que te lo den sin bolsa.

4. **Vas a visitar a un amigo que vive a un kilómetro de tu casa. ¿Cómo viajas?**
   a) Vas en autobús.
   b) Vas andando.
   c) Pides a tu padre que te lleve en coche.

5. **¿Cuáles de estos comestibles tienen más valor alimenticio?**
   a) La carne en lata.
   b) Las legumbres frescas.
   c) Las semillas de soya.

6. **Si construyeran una autopista cerca de tu casa, ¿qué harías?**
   a) Protestarías al gobierno municipal.
   b) Te mudarías de casa.
   c) Ahorrarías dinero para comprar un coche deportivo.

7. **¿Qué haces con un periódico después de leerlo?**
   a) Lo llevas a un centro de reciclaje para que pueda ser reutilizado.
   b) Lo echas a la basura.
   c) Lo guardas porque te puede servir para algo.

8. **Si tuvieras dinero, ¿qué tipo de abrigo te comprarías?**
   a) Un abrigo de cuero.
   b) Un abrigo de piel.
   c) Un abrigo de lana.

9. **¿Dónde prefieres vivir?**
   a) En un bloque de apartamentos en el centro de una ciudad.
   b) En una casa en un pueblo.
   c) En una tienda en el campo.

10. **Es de noche y estás solo(a) en casa. ¿Qué haces?**
    a) Miras la televisión, pero dejas todas las luces apagadas.
    b) Miras la televisión, pero enciendes todas las luces porque tienes miedo.
    c) Vas a mirar la televisión a la casa de un(a) amigo(a).

Minor adaptation of "Tú y el medio ambiente" from *Hoy Día*, vol. 32, no. 6, April/May 1990. Copyright © 1990 by **Scholastic, Inc.** Reprinted by permission of the publisher.

Holt Spanish 2 ¡Ven conmigo!, Chapter 11

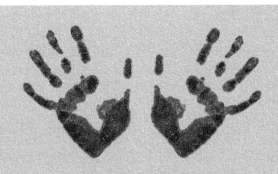

A LIMPIAR NUESTRO BELLO PLANETA TIERRA

No preguntes qué puedes hacer para conservar el medio ambiente. A todos nos toca reciclar, proteger las especies y conservar los recursos naturales.

La Fundación Alegría Verde tiene el gusto de invitarte a participar en nuestra campaña mundial para la limpieza de nuestro planeta. La campaña se va a realizar los días 19, 20 y 21 de septiembre.
Cada año miles de jóvenes de más de 200 países de todas las culturas y lenguas se dan cita en sus barrios, pueblos y ciudades durante estos tres días para limpiar un pedacito del planeta. La campaña culmina al atardecer del tercer día donde todos en nuestros respectivos países mandamos un abrazo al planeta y le decimos: ¡Te quiero planeta Tierra!

¡Ven! ¡Participa!

REALIA

REALIA

Realia 11-1: Endangered animals of Mexico

1. **Reading:** Have students read the article and find the following information:
   a. dirección de Internet
   b. las aves
   c. los animales de la selva

2. **Writing/Group work:** In groups of four, have students create an ad campaign like Pronatura's. They can choose an animal or place they want to protect and write a paragraph about the problem and how they plan to solve it. Each group needs to present its campaign to the class.

3. **Map:** In groups of three, have students find the places where the animals featured by Pronatura live. You may want to provide a map, or refer students to the map on page xxiii of the textbook.

4. **Culture:** The Galapagos Islands were once known as the Enchanted Islands because they disappeared into the fog at certain times of the year and sailors could not find them. Now this province of Ecuador is one of the world's most varied and interesting ecosystems. This chain of islands was never attached to any other land mass, so the species that populate the region are descended from ancestral species that flew, drifted, or swam there. As a result, the animals and plants that live on the islands are unique to this location. Some of the rare species one can find in the Galapagos are giant tortoises, penguins, albatrosses, fur seals, iguanas, and bats. Ask students if they can identify and describe an endangered species native to their area.

Realia 11-2: Tú y el medio ambiente

1. **Listening:** Ask students comprehension questions regarding the reading to make sure they understand the questionnaire.

2. **Reading:** Have students read the questionnaire and answer the questions to see how they rate.

3. **Speaking:** Have students discuss the results of the questionnaire. Ask them if they are ecological experts or if they need to learn more about the environment.

4. **Writing:** Have students in groups of three or four create their own questionnaire on environmental problems. First, have students think about an environmental topic of interest to the group or a combination of environmental topics. Then, have each group write five questions and include an evaluation. Students should use the questionnaire they answered as a model.

5. **Culture:** Costa Rica has made an exceptional effort to preserve its rain forest and natural resources. More than a quarter of the country has been set aside for conservation in the form of National Parks and Indian reserves. Many species of animals and plants that are threatened or extinct in neighboring countries still thrive in Costa Rica. To finance its conservation efforts, Costa Rica has signed a contract with Merck, a pharmaceutical company, to provide samples of plants and insect species in exchange for royalties from any marketable product. The hope is that scientists may be able to find cures for the most deadly diseases of our time, while preserving the forest.

Realia 11-3: Invitation to clean up the planet

1. **Reading:** Ask students to skim the article and find the following information:
   a. días de la campaña
   b. nombre de la organización
   c. propósito de la campaña

2. **Writing:** You may want to have students imagine they are the organizers of a clean-up activity. Have students write eight commands that summarize their program.

3. **Group work/Community:** In groups of four, have students attend a clean-up effort in their community. They should return to class and describe some of the tasks they did as part of that effort.

4. **Culture:** In Latin America and Spain there is a strong public interest in ecology. Schools and universities are involved in clean-up efforts similar to those in the United States. There is a growing awareness of the problems the planet is facing, and all countries are attempting new ways of protecting the environment. For example, public campaigns try to get people to recycle and not litter. Other efforts are geared to protect the rain forests through ecotourism and the sale of products that can be safely produced without endangering the ecosystem. For example, in Costa Rica there are efforts to harvest ornamental plants, raise iguanas, encourage ecotourism, and increase reforestation efforts. Ask your students to find out about clean-up efforts or environmental groups in their communities.

R E A L I A

Realia 12-1

Querida Ivickza:

¿Cómo estás? Te echo mucho de menos aquí en Cádiz. Papá y mamá están muy contentos con su nuevo apartamento en esta ciudad. No lo vas a creer, pero mi prima Zenia ya no está enojada conmigo. Gracias por tu consejo de escribirle una carta para aclarar las cosas. ¿Sigues trabajando tanto en la tienda de tus padres? Yo voy a quedarme en un albergue juvenil en la costa por una semana. ¿Sabías que mi tía Tere tiene novio? Se llama Pedro y es muy buena gente. Ellos piensan casarse en San Juan. Nosotros vamos a ir a la boda. Este fin de semana todos fuimos a comer a un restaurante cubano aquí cerca. El día anterior fuimos a ver una película de Jacobo Morales sobre Puerto Rico. ¡Echo mucho de menos al Caribe! Te veo en la boda de Tere y Pedro. Saludos a tus padres.

Con cariño,
Charo

P.D.
Este pequeño marcador de libros de la autora M.P. describe nuestra amistad.

Un buen amigo es... como un libro, siempre abierto a contestar preguntas.

Un buen amigo es... como el sol después de la tormenta.

Un buen amigo es... como un reloj, fiel, exacto y... a veces silencioso cuando lo necesitas.

FLAVIO CÉSAR
"fuera de serie"

Romántico por naturaleza, pensando siempre en el corazón de la gente que lo escucha. Flavio César

nos confesó...

Desde pequeño, Flavio tuvo esa inquietud de cantar, y su vocación se fue dando poco a poco hasta hoy, que además de ser cantante es artista: eso sí, siempre manteniendo un estilo original y auténtico, lo que para él es lo mejor que tiene. Él es muy sensible, alegre y soñador, pero muy, muy luchón. Esto lo ha llevado a lograr su más grande sueño.

En gustos se rompen géneros

Cuando le preguntamos sobre su comida favorita, hasta le brillaron los ojitos, y sin dudar ni un momento, contestó: "Adoro la comida mexicana", y nos confesó que es de bastante buen diente. Pero comer no es lo que más le gusta, prefiere el fútbol y practicar otro tipo de deportes.

Lo que nadie sabe

Así como lo ven de tierno y amigable, Flavio César también tiene su genio, pero no de los de las lámparas maravillosas, sino el que aflora cuando algo no le parece o cuando lo hacen enojar. Porque han de saber que es bastante perfeccionista y le gusta que todo salga como lo planea.

Cada vez está escalando más alto Flavio César, un artista joven y apasionado que quiere llegar al corazón de todos los que lo escuchan. Esta vez puso en su nuevo disco todo lo que él es, toda su evolución y todo su amor.

Muchas personas, en su mayoría mujeres, dicen que tiene un carisma muy especial y un ángel que lo hacen irresistible. Pero no sólo las mujeres hablan bien de él, en general todo el público que ha escuchado sus canciones queda satisfecho, porque opinan que su música es de lo más romántica, de ésas, de las que calan grueso hasta el alma.

Realia 12-3

TU FUTURO ESTÁ A LA VUELTA DE LA ESQUINA. SI NECESITAS DINERO Y TIENES MUCHOS SUEÑOS EL BANCO DE LA COMUNIDAD TE OFRECE LA CUENTA "JUVENTUD DIVINO TESORO". VEN Y HAZ REALIDAD TUS SUEÑOS DE:

- comprar un coche
- ir en el viaje de fin de curso a Europa
- pagar la matrícula para la universidad
- comprar una computadora

NUESTROS CONSEJOS PARA AYUDARTE SON FÁCILES ¡SÍGUELOS Y YA VERÁS!

1. Ahorra el dinero que te dan tus padres todos los meses.
2. Prepara tu merienda y tu almuerzo en casa.
3. Ve al cine sólo durante las horas de descuento.
4. Alquila videos que no sean estrenos.
5. Busca un trabajo a tiempo parcial.
6. Pide que te regalen dinero para tus cumpleaños y para las Navidades.

Tenemos la cuenta ideal reservada para ti. Ven a cualquiera de nuestras cien sucursales y empieza a ahorrar. Sólo necesitas $50.00 para abrir tu cuenta y cada mes ganarás un 5% de interés. Duplica tu dinero y abre las puertas al futuro.

REALIA

Realia 12-1: Letter with bookmark

1. **Reading:** Have students read the letter and, based on the poem, discuss the characteristics a good friend should have.

2. **Writing:** Students can write a letter to a friend telling them the latest news about themselves. You may want encourage students to use **Primer paso** vocabulary from page 371 of their textbook.

3. **Listening:** You may want to bring a series of photos to class and tell a story about where the people in each photo went and what they did. Have students take notes and be prepared to answer questions about the pictures.

4. **Culture:** Young people in Spain usually go on vacation together with their families. Their parents rent a place on the coast or vacation in the countryside. Others go with friends to different places in Europe and, since camping is not as popular as in the United States, they usually stay in **albergues juveniles**. These hostels are not very expensive and, although they are not always located in convenient places, they are the best alternatives for low-budget travel. Ask your students about their vacations. Do they vacation with friends or do they go with their families? Would they like to stay in an **albergue juvenil** or would they rather go camping?

Realia 12-2: Flavio César interview

1. **Reading:** Ask students to read the interview and make a list of the adjectives they find.

2. **Listening/Speaking:** Using Flavio César's interview as a model, have students work in groups of three to create a conversation between a well known talk show host, a famous artist, and an athlete. The conversation should focus on activities they like to do, a description of themselves, and what they would like to do on vacation. Each group uses their notes to present the conversation to the class by reading it to the class without revealing their names. Have the class guess the identities of the three members of each group.

3. **Pair work:** Ask students to bring a picture of someone and describe the person to the class. They can also talk about things the person likes, where he or she went last weekend, and this person's favorite pastimes.

4. **Culture:** In Spanish-speaking countries people often use terms of endearment when they're talking to someone they like a lot: for example, *Carlitos* for *Carlos*, and *Anita* for *Ana*. Grandchildren call their grandparents *abuelito/a* and their parents *mamita* and *papito*. Other words that they used frequently to refer to people they care about are **mi cielo** (*my darling*), **mi vida** (*my dear*) and **mi amor** (*my sweetheart*). **Mi hijo/a** doesn't necessarily refer to an actual son or daughter, but to a young person the speaker cares for. Ask students to list terms of endearment that people use in English.

Realia 12-3: Bank account ad

1. **Reading:** Have students read the article and say what it is about. Then, you may want students to choose three things they do to save money. Ask them what they plan to do with their savings in the future.

2. **Listening:** Read the advice given in Realia 12-3 about saving money and ask students if they believe it is good advice. Ask them to justify their opinion.

3. **Writing:** Ask students to imagine they are the president of a bank. Ask them to make a list of five things they feel would save money. They can use the list in Realia 12-3 as a model.

4. **Group work:** In groups of four, have students discuss their plans for the future. They can discuss where they will live, where they will study, and what they want to do after graduation.

5. **Culture:** Summer jobs are part of the activities young people can do during the summer months in the U.S. However, in Latin America, summer jobs are hard to find, so students cannot rely on them to save money. If a family member or friend happens to have a business, then there is a greater possibility of finding a job for the summer. Since jobs are often not an option, young people usually go on vacation with their parents, visit grandparents or other family members, or just spend some time with friends. Ask your students what they usually do for the summer. Do they work and save money? Do they go on vacation? What other summer options do they have?

Situation Cards

Situation Cards 1-1, 1-2, 1-3: Interview

Situation 1-1: Interview

Imagine you are at a party with a friend. How would you respond to the following questions?

¿Cómo te llamas y de dónde eres?

¿Cuántos años tienes?

¿Cómo se llama tu mejor amigo/a y de qué nacionalidad es?

¿Quieres conocer a los estudiantes paraguayos que están aquí?

¿Ya conoces a la muchacha de estatura mediana y de pelo castaño?

Situation 1-2: Interview

I am the President of the Spanish club that you want to join, and I am interviewing you to get to know you better. Respond to my questions:

¿Tocas algún instrumento o cantas?

¿Qué deportes practicas? ¿Te gusta nadar?

¿Adónde te gusta ir de paseo los fines de semana?

¿Tienes amigos que hablan español? ¿De qué nacionalidades son?

Situation 1-3: Interview

You and I have just been introduced. I am a foreign exchange student, and I would like to know more about your likes and dislikes. Answer these questions:

¿Te gusta estudiar? ¿Qué materias te gustan?

¿Qué haces los fines de semana?

¿Te encanta salir con tus amigos?

¿Qué tipo de música te gusta escuchar?

¿Con qué frecuencia te gusta escribir cartas?

SITUATION CARDS

Nombre _____ Clase _____ Fecha _____

  Situation Cards 1-1, 1-2, 1-3: Role-playing

Situation 1-1: Role-play

Student A   You and **Student B** exchange opinions about different teachers. Say whether you think a certain teacher is nice, friendly, smart, and so on. Give reasons why you like certain teachers.

Student B   You and **Student A** exchange opinions on different teachers. **Student A** will tell you what he or she thinks about certain teachers. Tell **Student A** whether you agree or disagree with his or her opinions.

Situation 1-2: Role-play

Student A   You want to get together with **Student B** sometime soon to do something. You ask **Student B** what he or she does after school, in the evening, and on the week-end. Try to find a time when you can both do a certain activity.

Student B   You want to get together with **Student A** sometime soon to do something. Answer **Student A's** questions by telling him or her what your schedule is like.

Situation 1-3: Role-play

Student A   You and **Student B** are preparing a video letter for your pen pal in South America. Ask each other questions about your favorite activities. Also describe some of your friends to your pen pal.

Student B   While preparing a video letter for a pen pal in South America, answer **Student A's** questions. Then ask him or her similar questions.

SITUATION CARDS

138 Activities for Communication

Holt Spanish 2 ¡Ven conmigo!, Chapter 1

Situation Cards 2-1, 2-2, 2-3: Interview

Situation 2-1: Interview

I am going to ask you about how you feel in different situations.
Respond to my questions.

¿Cómo te sientes cuando recibes una carta de un/a amigo/a?

¿Qué te pasa cuando no hay nada que hacer?

¿Cómo estás cuando vas a salir con tus amigos?

¿Cómo estás cuando tienes mucha tarea?

Situation 2-2: Interview

You are planning a welcome home party for a relative. I want to
help you, so I need to know what you have already prepared.
Answer my questions.

¿Ya mandaste las invitaciones?

¿Ya fuiste a comprar el pastel?

¿Terminaste con las decoraciones de la casa?

¿Quieres ayuda con la comida?

Situation 2-3: Interview

Imagine that we are best friends who haven't seen each other in
about a year. We finally get together and I ask you a lot of
questions. Respond to my questions.

¿Tu escuela está lejos o cerca de tu casa?

¿Cómo es tu ciudad en el invierno?

¿Cómo es el centro de la ciudad?

¿Qué tiempo hace en el verano?

¿Adónde vas con tus amigos los fines de semana?

SITUATION CARDS

Nombre _____ Clase _____ Fecha _____

 Situation Cards 2-1, 2-2, 2-3: Role-playing

Situation 2-1: Role-play

Student A You and **Student B** get together in the afternoon, but **Student B** seems bored. Suggest some activities for the two of you to do.

Student B You and **Student A** spend the afternoon together, but you are bored. **Student A** has some suggestions. How do you react to them?

Situation 2-2: Role-play

Student A You just returned from a trip to the beach. Ask **Student B** what she or he did over the weekend.

Student B You tell **Student A** about your dream date this past weekend. Also ask **Student A** about what he or she did at the beach.

¿Qué hiciste...? ¿Adónde fuiste...?
¿Cuántos fueron...?

Situation 2-3: Role-play

Student A You and **Student B** are planning to vacation at a resort. Ask **Student B** where you should go and then suggest a different place. Come to an agreement about where you will go.

Student B You and **Student A** are planning a trip to a resort. You have to agree on where to go. Suggest a place, then listen to **Student A**'s suggestions. Come to an agreement about where you will go.

SITUATION CARDS

Holt Spanish 2 ¡Ven conmigo!, Chapter 2

Situation 3-1: Interview

You are with your host family in Puerto Rico for the first time. Your host mother asks you about your daily routine. How would you answer the following questions?

Por lo general, ¿cuánto tiempo gastas en vestirte?
¿Cuándo te bañas?, ¿por la noche o por la mañana?
En general, ¿a qué hora te levantas por la mañana?
¿Cuántas veces a la semana te lavas el pelo?

Situation 3-2: Interview

On the refrigerator door there is a list of chores that you need to do today. Which items have you already done?

¿Ya sacaste la basura?
¿Ordenaste tu cuarto?
¿Limpiaste el cuarto de baño?
¿Pasaste la aspiradora esta semana?

Situation 3-3: Interview

Your school paper wants to publish a survey on students' hobbies. A classmate who works for the paper asks you some questions.

¿Cuál es tu pasatiempo favorito?
¿Cuánto tiempo hace que lo practicas?
¿Cuáles pasatiempos no te gustan?
¿Prefieres los deportes, los juegos de mesa o los videojuegos?

SITUATION CARDS

Nombre _____ Clase _____ Fecha _____

 Situation Cards 3-1, 3-2, 3-3: Role-playing

Situation 3-1: Role-play

Student A   You are a talk show host and **Student B** is a famous celebrity. Ask **Student B** his or her name. Then ask **Student B** about his or her daily routine and what he or she likes to do.

Student B   You are a famous celebrity and **Student A** is the host of a talk show. **Student A** will interview you and ask you some personal questions. Answer **Student A**'s questions.

Situation 3-2: Role-play

Student A   You and a friend, **Student B**, are planning a party. Ask **Student B** to help you do the following chores: dust the living room, vacuum, and sweep the kitchen floor. When **Student B** asks you to do other chores, make sure you complain.

Student B   You and a friend, **Student A**, are planning a party. Ask **Student A** to help you with some of the chores: clean the bathroom, dust, and mow the lawn. Make sure you complain when **Student A** asks you to do other chores.

Situation 3-3: Role-play

Student A   Ask **Student B** about what activities he or she enjoys doing on the weekends. Find out how long **Student B** has been doing those activities and what other activities he or she would like to do.

Student B   Answer **Student A**'s questions about your weekend activities. Be sure to include how long you've been doing those activities. Answer any other questions that **Student A** may have.

SITUATION CARDS

142 Activities for Communication

Holt Spanish 2 ¡Ven conmigo!, Chapter 3

Nombre _____ Clase _____ Fecha _____

Situation Cards 4-1, 4-2, 4-3: Interviews

Situation 4-1: Interview

Imagine that the school counselor has called you into the office to ask you a few questions. How would you answer these questions?

¿Qué te parece la clase de español?
¿Crees que cometes muchos errores?
En tu opinión, ¿es importante hacer preguntas cuando no entiendes algo?
¿Siempre prestas atención? ¿Por qué o por qué no?

Situation 4-2: Interview

A new student at school wants to know about one of the Spanish teachers. How would you respond to these questions?

¿Conoces a la profesora (al profesor) _____?
¿Es muy exigente? ¿Es justo/a?
¿Es mejor que los otros profesores?
¿Hay que estudiar mucho para sacar una buena nota en su clase?

Situation 4-3: Interview

You and one of your friends are making plans to go out after school. How would you respond to your friend's questions?

Pienso ir al cine esta tarde. ¿Quieres venir?
¿Quieres mirar las vitrinas de las tiendas antes de hacer cola?
¿Qué te parece si cenamos antes de ir al cine?
¿Quieres salir con otros amigos después de ir al cine?
Entonces paso por ti a las cinco. ¿Está bien?

Holt Spanish 2 ¡Ven conmigo!, Chapter 4   Activities for Communication **143**
Copyright © by Holt, Rinehart and Winston. All rights reserved.

Situation Cards 4-1, 4-2, 4-3: Role-playing

Situation 4-1: Role-play

Student A You are a late night radio talk show host who has good advice for any type of problem. **Student B** calls the station. Listen to **Student B** describe his or her problem and offer some advice.

Student B You call **Student A**, a late night talk show host, about the problems you have encountered since you transferred to your new school. Mention some problems you have encountered so far and ask **Student A** for some advice.

Situation 4-2: Role-play

Student A Ask **Student B** what qualities he or she thinks make a good student. Then answer **Student B**'s questions.

Student B **Student A** is going to interview you regarding the habits that make a successful student. Answer his or her questions. Then ask **Student A**'s opinions about what it takes to be a good student.

Situation 4-3: Role-play

Student A Imagine that **Student B** is a new student in your class. Find out how difficult **Student B**'s old school is compared to yours. Be sure to use comparisons.

Student B Imagine that you are a new student in this school. **Student A** wants to you to compare your old school with the new one. Answer **Student A**'s questions.

peor que   mejor que   más ... que   menos ... que

SITUATION CARDS

Holt Spanish 2 ¡Ven conmigo!, Chapter 4

Situation 5-1: Interview

Your gym teacher has asked you to come in the office to ask you a few questions. How would you respond?

¿Qué haces para estar en plena forma?
¿Prefieres levantar pesas o prefieres la natación?
¿Duermes lo suficiente todos los días?
¿Qué es preciso hacer para estar sano(a)?

Situation 5-2: Interview

Your friend asks you for advice on how to lead a more healthy life. How would you respond?

¿Qué debo hacer para ponerme en forma?
¿Qué haces tú para relajarte?
En tu opinión, ¿qué es un hábito malo?
¿Qué debo hacer para evitar el estrés?

Situation 5-3: Interview

Your exercise partner is wondering why you didn't come to the gym last night. How would you respond?

¿Por qué no pasaste por el gimnasio ayer?
¿Te lastimaste? ¿Qué te pasó?
¿Por qué te quejas tanto?

SITUATION CARDS

Situation Cards 5-1, 5-2, 5-3: Role-playing

Situation 5-1: Role-play

Student A   You are a reporter for the school newspaper and you have been asked to collect opinions about different lifestyles at the school's health fair. Ask **Student B,** who is visiting the health fair, how he or she thinks people can keep fit. Then ask questions on how he or she keeps fit.

Student B   You are visiting the school's annual health fair. A reporter from the school newspaper (**Student A**) stops you and asks you a few questions. Answer his or her questions.

Situation 5-2: Role-play

Student A   You are a doctor and your patient (**Student B**) has not been feeling well lately. Ask **Student B** about his or her everyday habits and eating preferences. Recommend changes for **Student B** in order to prevent any further problems.

Student B   You are a patient who hasn't been feeling well. Your doctor (**Student A**) is asking you about your everyday habits and eating preferences. Answer **Student A's** questions.

Situation 5-3: Role-play

Student A   You and your exercise partner (**Student B**) are supposed to work out at the gym together, but you need to cancel tonight's workout. Call **Student B** and tell him or her that you need to cancel and explain why.

Student B   Your exercise partner (**Student A**) has just called you to tell you why he or she is not going to work out this evening. You really don't want to miss this workout because **Student A** has already cancelled once this week. Try to convince your partner to go.

SITUATION CARDS

Situation Cards 6-1, 6-2, 6-3: Interview

Situation 6-1: Interview

You are working at the information desk of the bureau of tourism in your city and I am a new visitor. Answer my questions to help me get around the city.

Disculpe, ¿conoce Ud. bien la ciudad? ¿Tiene un mapa que pueda darme?

¿Sabe si hay un guía que me pueda ayudar?

¿Me podría decir dónde está la parada del autobús?

¿Sabe si hay un museo por aquí?

Situation 6-2: Interview

Imagine you have recently returned from a trip. I am curious about what you did. Answer my questions.

Primero, ¿adónde fuiste?

A continuación, ¿qué hiciste?

Después, ¿dónde comiste?

Luego, ¿qué más hiciste?

Por último, ¿qué te gustó más?

Situation 6-3: Interview

Imagine you are at a restaurant and I am your server. Answer my questions and respond to my suggestions.

¿Ya sabe qué va a pedir? Recomiendo la especialidad de la casa, hamburguesas con papas fritas.

Y, ¿qué le traigo de tomar?

¿Qué desea de postre?

¿Se le ofrece algo más?

SITUATION CARDS

Situation Cards 6-1, 6-2, 6-3: Role-playing

Situation 6-1: Role-play

Student A   You are a tourist in San Antonio. You want to see the sites, so you stop **Student B** and ask questions regarding different tourist attractions. **Student B** will help you find your way around the city.

Student B   **Student A** is a tourist in San Antonio. He or she wants to see some tourist attractions and stops you to ask you questions. Answer **Student A**'s questions. You may use the map on p. 147 of the textbook for help.

Situation 6-2: Role-play

Student A   You are hosting **Student B**, an exchange student from Ecuador. **Student B** is eager to visit your city. **Student B** will ask you about your favorite places to visit and how you can get around. Plan a day trip and state in what order you will visit places.

Student B   You are an exchange student from Ecuador visiting San Antonio for the first time. **Student A** is your host sister or brother. You are eager to visit the tourist attractions. Ask **Student A** how to get there and the order in which you will visit those places.

Situation 6-3: Role-play

Student A   You are writing an article for a well-known gourmet magazine. You know **Student B** went to a restaurant you need to include in your article. Ask **Student B** what everybody in his or her party ordered and how much of a tip they left.

Student B   You have recently eaten at a famous restaurant. **Student A** is writing an article for a gourmet magazine and will ask you questions about what you ordered and how much of a tip you left. Answer **Student A**'s questions.

SITUATION CARDS

Situation Cards 7-1, 7-2, 7-3: Interview

Situation 7-1: Interview

Imagine you are a famous singer from the Caribbean. I am writing an interview on you for a teen magazine. I am going to ask you a few questions about your past that your fans are very curious about.

Cuando eras joven, ¿tenías un apodo? ¿Cuál era?
¿Dónde vivías cuando tenías ocho años?
De pequeño/a, ¿qué pasatiempo te gustaba?
De niño/a, ¿te gustaba hacer travesuras?

Situation 7-2: Interview

I am a new friend that just moved into the neighborhood. I am curious to find out how the neighborhood has changed since you were younger.

En aquellos tiempos, ¿cómo era donde vivías ?
¿Cómo era tu escuela en aquel entonces?
¿Qué tipo de juegos jugabas en aquel entonces?
¿Cómo eran los otros niños que jugaban contigo en aquella época?

Situation 7-3: Interview

You are having lunch and I come over to join you. I begin asking you some questions about some classmates. Answer my questions as best you can without taking sides by using comparisons of equality.

¿Quién es la estudiante más simpática de tu clase?
¿Quién es el estudiante mas egoísta de tu clase?
¿Quién crees tú que es tan feliz como una lombriz en tu clase?

SITUATION CARDS

Situation Cards 7-1, 7-2, 7-3: Role-playing

Situation 7-1: Role-play

Student A   You are a reporter for the school paper. You need to find out what students did on the weekends when they were younger (between ages 8–10). Interview **Student B** and ask **Student B** questions about the things he or she did at that age on the weekends.

Student B   **Student A** is a reporter for the school newspaper and is going to interview you regarding the things you did on the weekends when you were younger. Answer **Student A**'s questions.

Situation 7-2: Role-play

Student A   **Student B** is a visitor from the past. You are very curious to find out how things were then. Ask **Student B** questions about the past. Make sure you ask **Student B** about the city, the neighborhood and some of the people that still live there.

Student B   You have just traveled 30 years ahead in time. **Student A** wants to know about the city, some of the people that are still alive in the neighborhood, and the neighborhood itself. Answer **Student A**'s questions.

Situation 7-3: Role-play

Student A   Imagine that you are visiting your grandparent, **Student B**. Ask him or her to tell you about his or her school and to compare it to your school now.

Student B   Imagine that you are **Student A**'s grandparent. **Student A** is going to ask you about your school and also wants you to compare it to school now. Answer **Student A**'s questions.

S I T U A T I O N   C A R D S

Nombre _____ Clase _____ Fecha _____

Situation Cards 8-1, 8-2, 8-3: Interview

Situation 8-1: Interview

You have just attended the grand opening of a new theme park. As you are leaving, a reporter stops and asks you some questions about your visit.

¿Qué tal estuvo el estreno del parque de atracciones?
¿Te divertiste en la montaña rusa?
¿Visitaste el zoológico que también abrió hoy?
¿Cómo te fue en la rueda de Chicago y los carros chocones?

Situation 8-2: Interview

Your friend calls and asks you why you couldn't get together to do something last weekend. Answer these questions.

¿Por qué no asististe a la fiesta el viernes pasado?
Fui al café el sábado pasado. ¿Por qué no fuiste tú?
¿Cuáles quehaceres o mandados tenías que hacer mientras nosotros íbamos al estreno?

Situation 8-3: Interview

Imagine that a close friend went to the festival **el Día de las Máscaras** last December. Answer these questions.

¿Qué te dijo tu amigo/a del festival?
¿Te dijo si le gustaron las máscaras?
¿Qué te dijo de los desfiles?
¿Te dijo si disfrutó su viaje?

SITUATION CARDS

Nombre _____ Clase _____ Fecha _____

 Situation Cards 8-1, 8-2, 8-3: Role-playing

Situation 8-1: Role-play

Student A   You have asked **Student B** to lunch so that you can find out how the premiere of the new movie was last week. Ask **Student B** questions about this exciting event.

Student B   **Student A** has asked you to lunch to find out about the premiere of the new hit movie you attended last week. Answer **Student A**'s questions.

Situation 8-2: Role-play

Student A   You were scheduled to meet some friends for lunch but you couldn't go because you had a lot of things to do. **Student B** is calling to find out what happened to you. Explain to **Student B** what errands you needed to do.

Student B   You and some friends met for lunch but **Student A** never showed up. Call **Student A** and ask why she or he wasn't able to come.

Situation 8-3: Role-play

Student A   You were sick and unable to make it to Spanish class, so you call **Student B** to find out what your Spanish teacher said about the **Día de las Máscaras** festival in Puerto Rico. Ask **Student B** what your teacher said.

Student B   Your Spanish teacher gave a great lecture on the **Día de las Máscaras** festival in Puerto Rico. **Student A** was sick and unable to make it to Spanish class and has just called you to find out what your teacher said. Answer **Student A**'s questions.

SITUATION CARDS

Nombre _____ Clase _____ Fecha _____

Situation 9-1: Interview

You are working in the tourist information office in Cuenca, Ecuador. Using the map on page 225 of your textbook, answer my questions.

Disculpe, ¿dónde queda el Museo de Artes Populares?
Perdón, ¿me puede decir dónde está el restaurante Claro de Luna?
Disculpe, ¿dónde hay un hotel cerca del aeropuerto?
¿Me puede decir dónde está el correo?

Situation 9-2: Interview

You are a customer in a store, and I am the salesclerk. You want to buy some new clothes. Respond to these questions.

¿En qué le puedo servir?
¿Qué talla necesita?
¿Cómo le queda la camisa?
¿Le traigo alguna otra cosa?
¿Cómo quiere pagar?

Situation 9-3: Interview

You're in charge of the school yard sale to raise funds for the school prom. Answer my questions. Try to drive a hard bargain.

¿Cuánto valen estos libros?
¿En cuánto me los dejas?
¿Qué precio tiene la mochila?
Los cuadernos cuestan una fortuna. ¿Me puedes rebajar el precio?
¿No los puedes vender más baratos?

SITUATION CARDS

Situation Cards 9-1, 9-2, 9-3: Role-playing

Situation 9-1: Role-play

Student A   You have invited **Student B** to a party at your house on Saturday. **Student B** calls you to find out how to get from school to your house. Answer **Student B**'s questions and tell him or her exactly how to get to your house from school.

Student B   You are going to a party at **Student A**'s house on Saturday. You call **Student A** to find out exactly where he or she lives. When you have all the directions, repeat them to **Student A** to make sure you got them right.

Situation 9-2: Role-play

Student A   You are a customer at a boutique in Lima, Peru, and **Student B** is the salesclerk. Ask **Student B** for help with the clothes you want to buy. Ask **Student B** where you can try on the clothes. Finally, ask **Student B** to tell you how the clothes look on you.

Student B   You are a salesclerk in a boutique in Lima, Peru. **Student A** is a customer who wants to buy some clothes. Help **Student A** decide what to buy, and answer **Student A**'s questions.

Situation 9-3: Role-play

Student A   You have your own booth at an open-air market in Santiago de Chile. You sell clothes, shoes, and everything you can think of. **Student B** is a customer who wants the best possible price. You are willing to give **Student B** a 50% discount, provided that **Student B** buys a lot of merchandise. **Student B** will bargain with you.

Student B   You are a wise shopper at an open-air market in Santiago de Chile. **Student A** is the salesperson. Be prepared to bargain with **Student A**.

SITUATION CARDS

Situation Cards 10-1, 10-2, 10-3: Interview

Situation 10-1: Interview

You are working as a teacher's aide at a day care center. It is your turn to tell the children a story. Answer the day care teacher's questions about the story or legend you will tell the children so that she or he can determine whether it is appropriate.

¿Cómo empieza el cuento?
¿Describe el tiempo de las primeras escenas del cuento?
¿Describe lo que la gente hacía y cómo se sentía?
¿Es un cuento de misterio, de amor, de aventura o de ciencia ficción?

Situation 10-2: Interview

You have just written a science fiction story, and I want to help you make sure it follows a logical sequence. I will ask you questions to help you tell the story better. Respond to my questions.

¿Cómo comienza el cuento?
¿Qué pasa entonces?
¿Qué pasó de repente?
¿Qué pasó al final?
En fin, ¿cómo salió todo?

Situation 10-3: Interview

You and your friends are talking about a very difficult surprise test in Spanish class. Answer your friends' questions.

Oye, ¿has oído hablar del examen de español?
¿Te enteraste que va a ser muy difícil?
Fíjate, me dijeron que nadie lo puede pasar. ¿Qué crees tú?
Oye, ¿no sabes cuándo va a dar el examen?

SITUATION CARDS

Situation Cards 10-1, 10-2, 10-3: Role-playing

Situation 10-1: Role-play

Student A   **Student B** wants to write a mystery short story and has asked for help in setting the scene. Ask **Student B** to describe some of the things the characters were doing and/or feeling. **Student B** will ask you to describe what the weather was like.

Student B   You want to write a mystery short story and you have asked **Student A** to help set the scene. **Student A** will ask you to describe some things the characters were doing and/or feeling. Ask **Student A** to describe what the weather was like.

Situation 10-2: Role-play

Student A   **Student B** will begin a story and ask you to continue and end it. Then you will begin a story and ask **Student B** to continue and end it.

Student B   You will begin a story and ask **Student A** to continue and end it. Then, **Student A** will begin a story and ask you to continue and end it.

Situation 10-3: Role-play

Student A   Tell **Student B** some news or gossip and listen to **Student B** react to what you tell him or her. **Student B** will then tell you some news or gossip and you must react to the news.

Student B   **Student A** will tell you some news or gossip and you must react to the news. Then you will tell **Student A** some news or gossip and listen for his or her reaction.

Situation Cards 11-1, 11-2, 11-3: Interview

Situation 11-1: Interview

You are interested in joining the Ecology Club at school and need to be interviewed by the new members' committee to see if you have the same concerns as the other members. Respond to the committee's questions.

En tu opinión, ¿cuál es el problema más grave del medio ambiente?

¿Cómo crees que se puede mejorar la situación?

¿Qué haces tú para no desperdiciar los recursos naturales?

¿Qué opinas de la selva tropical?

¿Cómo crees que se puede mejorar el medio ambiente?

Situation 11-2: Interview

You and some friends are talking about the environment. One of your friends is trying to convince you that there are no problems with the environment. Respond to these questions.

¿Por qué es urgente enfrentar la crisis del medio ambiente?

¡Te equivocas! ¿Qué desperdicios hacemos?

Mira..., ¿no crees que tenemos que poner más carros y autobuses para mejorar el sistema de transportación?

¿Cómo vamos a vender comida y productos si no los empacamos?

¿Por qué estás preocupado/a por las selvas tropicales? Allí las cosas crecen rápidamente.

Situation 11-3: Interview

Your school newspaper is writing a feature article on Earth Day and you have been selected as a typical student for an interview. Respond to the reporter's questions.

¿Qué es más importante, reciclar o conservar energía?

¿Evitas los productos empacados?

¿Cuál va a ser el efecto si todos dejamos de comprar productos empacados?

¿Por qué no tenemos un sistema para mantener limpia la ciudad?

¿Cómo crees que podemos resolver todo?

SITUATION CARDS

Situation Cards 11-1, 11-2, 11-3: Role-playing

Situation 11-1: Role-play

Student A As a member of the school's Ecology Club, you and **Student B** must prepare a list of three or four environmental or ecological problems that your club will work on this year. Your list should include a description of each problem you both decide upon.

Student B As a member of the school's Ecology Club, you and **Student A** must prepare a list of three or four environmental or ecological problems that your club will work on this year. Your list should include a description of each problem you both decide upon.

Situation 11-2: Role-play

Student A Choose the environmental or ecological problem that you feel is the worst and try to convince **Student B** about the consequences to our environment if this problem is not solved. **Student B** will try to convince you that there is another problem that is greater. Agree or disagree with **Student B**.

Student B Listen to **Student A** talk about what he or she feels is the worst environmental or ecological problem we have and its consequences. Disagree with **Student A** and talk about another environmental or ecological problem that you feel has greater consequences.

Situation 11-3: Role-play

Student A Describe an environmental problem to **Student B** and ask for a possible solution. After **Student B** gives you some solutions or obligations he or she will describe to you a different environmental problem. You should give **Student B** some solutions.

Student B **Student A** will describe an environmental problem to you and ask you for a possible solution. Give **Student A** some solutions or obligations to the problem he or she has described. Then you will describe a different environmental problem and ask **Student A** for a possible solution.

SITUATION CARDS